D1712454

Karen Horney

Karen Horney

CONSTANCE JONES

CHELSEA HOUSE PUBLISHERS

NEW YORK · PHILADELPHIA

92
Horney
J

Chelsea House Publishers
EDITOR-IN-CHIEF Nancy Toff
EXECUTIVE EDITOR Remmel T. Nunn
MANAGING EDITOR Karyn Gullen Browne
COPY CHIEF Juliann Barbato
PICTURE EDITOR Adrian G. Allen
ART DIRECTOR Maria Epes
MANUFACTURING MANAGER Gerald Levine

American Women of Achievement
SENIOR EDITOR Constance Jones

Staff for KAREN HORNEY
COPY EDITOR Philip Koslow
DEPUTY COPY CHIEF Nicole Bowen
EDITORIAL ASSISTANT Claire Wilson
PICTURE RESEARCHER Joan Beard
ASSISTANT ART DIRECTOR Loraine Machlin
DESIGNER Donna Sinisgalli
PRODUCTION COORDINATOR Joseph Romano
COVER SCULPTURE Hilda Shen
COVER PHOTOGRAPH Sarah Lewis
COVER PAINTING Michelle Brisson

First Printing

1 3 5 7 9 8 6 4 2

Library of Congress Cataloging-in-Publication Data

Jones, Constance.
  Karen Horney.

  (American women of achievement)
  Bibliography: p.
  Includes index.
  1. Horney, Karen, 1855–1932.   2. Psychoanalysts—
United States—Biography.   I. Title.   II. Series.
RC438.6.H67J66   1989   150.19′5′0924 [B] 88-35366
ISBN 1-55546-659-1
     0-7910-0438-4 (pbk.)

CONTENTS

AMERICAN WOMEN OF ACHIEVEMENT

Abigail Adams
women's rights advocate

Jane Addams
social worker

Louisa May Alcott
author

Marian Anderson
singer

Susan B. Anthony
woman suffragist

Ethel Barrymore
actress

Clara Barton
*founder of the American
Red Cross*

Elizabeth Blackwell
physician

Nellie Bly
journalist

Margaret Bourke-White
photographer

Pearl Buck
author

Rachel Carson
biologist and author

Mary Cassatt
artist

Agnes De Mille
choreographer

Emily Dickinson
poet

Isadora Duncan
dancer

Amelia Earhart
aviator

Mary Baker Eddy
*founder of the Christian
Science church*

Betty Friedan
feminist

Althea Gibson
tennis champion

Emma Goldman
political activist

Helen Hayes
actress

Lillian Hellman
playwright

Katharine Hepburn
actress

Karen Horney
psychoanalyst

Anne Hutchinson
religious leader

Mahalia Jackson
gospel singer

Helen Keller
humanitarian

Jeane Kirkpatrick
diplomat

Emma Lazarus
poet

Clare Boothe Luce
author and diplomat

Barbara McClintock
biologist

Margaret Mead
anthropologist

Edna St. Vincent Millay
poet

Julia Morgan
architect

Grandma Moses
painter

Louise Nevelson
sculptor

Sandra Day O'Connor
Supreme Court justice

Georgia O'Keeffe
painter

Eleanor Roosevelt
diplomat and humanitarian

Wilma Rudolph
champion athlete

Florence Sabin
medical researcher

Beverly Sills
opera singer

Gertrude Stein
author

Gloria Steinem
feminist

Harriet Beecher Stowe
author and abolitionist

Mae West
entertainer

Edith Wharton
author

Phillis Wheatley
poet

Babe Didrikson Zaharias
champion athlete

CHELSEA HOUSE PUBLISHERS

"REMEMBER THE LADIES"

MATINA S. HORNER

Remember the Ladies." That is what Abigail Adams wrote to her husband, John, then a delegate to the Continental Congress, as the Founding Fathers met in Philadelphia to form a new nation in March of 1776. "Be more generous and favorable to them than your ancestors. Do not put such unlimited power in the hands of the Husbands. If particular care and attention is not paid to the Ladies," Abigail Adams warned, "we are determined to foment a Rebellion, and will not hold ourselves bound by any Laws in which we have no voice, or Representation."

The words of Abigail Adams, one of the earliest American advocates of women's rights, were prophetic. Because when we have not "remembered the ladies," they have, by their words and deeds, reminded us so forcefully of the omission that we cannot fail to remember them. For the history of American women is as interesting and varied as the history of our nation as a whole. American women have played an integral part in founding, settling, and building our country. Some we remember as remarkable women who—against great odds—achieved distinction in the public arena: Anne Hutchinson, who in the 17th century became a charismatic religious leader; Phillis Wheatley, an 18th-century black slave who became a poet; Susan B. Anthony, whose name is synonymous with the 19th-century women's rights movement and who led the struggle to enfranchise women; and, in our own century, Amelia Earhart, the first woman to cross the Atlantic Ocean by air.

7

These extraordinary women certainly merit our admiration, but other women, "common women," many of them all but forgotten, should also be recognized for their contributions to American thought and culture. Women have been community builders; they have founded schools and formed voluntary associations to help those in need; they have assumed the major responsibility for rearing children, passing on from one generation to the next the values that keep a culture alive. These and innumerable other contributions, once ignored, are now being recognized by scholars, students, and the public. It is exciting and gratifying to realize that a part of our history that was hardly acknowledged a few generations ago is now being studied and brought to light.

In recent decades, the field of women's history has grown from obscurity to a politically controversial splinter movement to academic respectability, in many cases mainstreamed into such traditional disciplines as history, economics, and psychology. Scholars of women, both female and male, have organized research centers at such prestigious institutions as Wellesley College, Stanford University, and the University of California. Other notable centers for women's studies are the Center for the American Woman and Politics at the Eagleton Institute of Politics at Rutgers University; the Henry A. Murray Research Center for the Study of Lives, at Radcliffe College; and the Women's Research and Education Institute, the research arm of the Congressional Caucus on Women's Issues. Other scholars and public figures have established archives and libraries, such as the Schlesinger Library on the History of Women in America, at Radcliffe College, and the Sophia Smith Collection, at Smith College, to collect and preserve the written and tangible legacies of women.

From the initial donation of the Women's Rights Collection in 1943, the Schlesinger Library grew to encompass vast collections documenting the manifold accomplishments of American women. Simultaneously, the women's movement in general and the academic discipline of women's studies in particular also began with a narrow definition and gradually expanded their mandate. Early causes such as woman suffrage and social reform, abolition and organized labor were joined by newer concerns such as the history of women in business and the professions and in politics and government; the study of the family; and social issues such as health policy and education.

Women, as historian Arthur M. Schlesinger, jr., once pointed out, "have constituted the most spectacular casualty of traditional history.

They have made up at least half the human race, but you could never tell that by looking at the books historians write." The new breed of historians is remedying that omission. They have written books about immigrant women and about working-class women who struggled for survival in cities and about black women who met the challenges of life in rural areas. They are telling the stories of women who, despite the barriers of tradition and economics, became lawyers and doctors and public figures.

The women's studies movement has also led scholars to question traditional interpretations of their respective disciplines. For example, the study of war has traditionally been an exercise in military and political analysis, an examination of strategies planned and executed by men. But scholars of women's history have pointed out that wars have also been periods of tremendous change and even opportunity for women, because the very absence of men on the home front enabled them to expand their educational, economic, and professional activities and to assume leadership in their homes.

The early scholars of women's history showed a unique brand of courage in choosing to investigate new subjects and take new approaches to old ones. Often, like their subjects, they endured criticism and even ostracism by their academic colleagues. But their efforts have unquestionably been worthwhile, because with the publication of each new study and book another piece of the historical patchwork is sewn into place, revealing an increasingly comprehensive picture of the role of women in our rich and varied history.

Such books on groups of women are essential, but books that focus on the lives of individuals are equally indispensable. Biographies can be inspirational, offering their readers the example of people with vision who have looked outside themselves for their goals and have often struggled against great obstacles to achieve them. Marian Anderson, for instance, had to overcome racial bigotry in order to perfect her art and perform as a concert singer. Isadora Duncan defied the rules of classical dance to find true artistic freedom. Jane Addams had to break down society's notions of the proper role for women in order to create new social institutions, notably the settlement house. All of these women had to come to terms both with themselves and with the world in which they lived. Only then could they move ahead as pioneers in their chosen callings.

Biography can inspire not only by adulation but also by realism. It helps us to see not only the qualities in others that we hope to emulate but also, perhaps, the weaknesses that made them "human." By helping us identify with the subject on a more personal level they help us to feel that we, too, can achieve such goals. We read about Eleanor Roosevelt, for example, who occupied a unique and seemingly enviable position as the wife of the president. Yet we can sympathize with her inner dilemma: an inherently shy woman who had to force herself to live a most public life in order to use her position to benefit others. We may not be able to imagine ourselves having the immense poetic talent of Emily Dickinson, but from her story we can understand the challenges faced by a creative woman who was expected to fulfill many family responsibilities. And though few of us will ever reach the level of athletic accomplishment displayed by Wilma Rudolph or Babe Zaharias, we can still appreciate their spirit, their overwhelming will to excel.

A biography is a multifaceted lens. It is first of all a magnification, the intimate examination of one particular life. But at the same time, it is a wide-angle lens, informing us about the world in which the subject lived. We come away from reading about one life knowing more about the social, political, and economic fabric of the time. It is for this reason, perhaps, that the great New England essayist Ralph Waldo Emerson wrote, in 1841, "There is properly no history: only biography." And it is also why biography, and particularly women's biography, will continue to fascinate writers and readers alike.

Karen Horney

Psychoanalyst Karen Horney proposed dramatic revisions of Sigmund Freud's theory of human psychology. Many of her scientific peers greeted her ideas with skepticism or hostility.

ONE

New Ways

On the evening of April 29, 1941, the members of the New York Psychoanalytic Society and Institute gathered for their annual business meeting. The 60 scientists were among the pioneers who had introduced *psychoanalysis*, a radical new theory of human psychology, to the United States. A decade of struggle had earned this fledgling branch of psychiatry growing respect from the American medical establishment. Now the New York group, which included many of the leaders of that effort, met to determine the course of its work for the coming year. After nominating the officers who would direct the research and teaching efforts of the institute, the society heard a report from one of its members.

Dr. Gregory Zilboorg, chair of the committee that oversaw the institute's instruction of young psychoanalysts, read a resolution passed by the committee three weeks earlier. The statement asserted the importance of teaching psychoanalysis only in the form developed by its creator, Sigmund Freud. According to the committee, students should not be exposed to criticisms of Freud's ideas until they had thoroughly learned his basic principles. Most attempts to revise psychoanalytic theory, announced the committee, lacked value and would only mislead beginning students. The report went on to state that some of the institute's faculty were guilty of teaching such "impure" theory. "The published writings and contentions of Dr. Karen Horney present, in this respect, a case in point," Zilboorg declared, reaching the heart of the resolution. "The Education Committee has therefore decided to change the status of Dr. Karen Horney from that of Instructor to that of Lecturer, effective at the end of this academic year."

Karen Horney (pronounced *horn-eye*), seated with her colleagues in the auditorium, was outraged at the attack and insulted by the move to demote her. Born and educated in Germany, which bordered Sigmund Freud's native Austria, she had been one of the first practitioners trained in psychoanalytic technique. She had helped devise the methods by which analysts were now educated, and she had conducted ground-breaking psychological research. A founding member of the first American psychoanalytic institute, chartered in 1932 in Chicago, Illinois, Horney was one of the most experienced analysts in the United States. Her bold critiques of psychoanalytic theory, however, had angered those who believed that Freudian doctrine needed no improvement. Now, Horney listened in stunned silence while the assembled analysts—many of whom she had trained herself—debated whether she should be allowed to continue teaching newcomers to the field.

Horney's supporters argued strongly against the proposal before it was submitted to a vote. The balloting revealed the deep divisions within the society: Twenty-nine members abstained from voting because, although most of them supported Horney's right to develop and teach her theories, they were too timid to challenge the society's leadership by voting against the committee's proposal. Of those who did cast ballots, 24 came out in favor of the motion to demote Horney, and 7 against. Horney would no longer be permitted to train new students, although she could continue lecturing experienced analysts.

Horney was accustomed to being the focus of controversy, but this decision was hard for her to accept. There was only one way, she felt, to respond to the vindictive actions of those who feared and resented her. While the hushed assembly watched, the dignified, graying doctor rose from her seat and, without saying a word, walked slowly up the aisle and out the door. Four of her colleagues followed, leaving behind the dumbstruck members of the New York Psychoanalytic Society and Institute. Before that evening, no member had ever dared protest any action of the New York Psychoanalytic in such a dramatic fashion. After that evening, according to Harold Kelman, one of Horney's associates, "Psychoanalysis as a movement was never the same. . . ."

The events of April 29, 1941, represented the culmination of a battle that had raged at the institute for nearly two years. In the summer of 1939, Horney had published her second book, *New Ways in Psychoanalysis*. A bold appraisal of the strengths and weaknesses of Freudian theory, the volume questioned the validity of many of the central precepts of psychoanalysis. Horney knew that the book would upset many analysts, even though she explained in the introduction that "the purpose of this book is not to show what is wrong with psychoanalysis." Indeed, she recognized the brilliance of many

Freudian concepts, ideas that had revolutionized 20th-century psychology. But Horney felt that psychoanalytic theory was flawed, and she hoped that "through eliminating the debatable elements," she could "enable psychoanalysis to develop to the height of its potentialities."

Each chapter of *New Ways in Psychoanalysis* examined one of the fundamental principles of Freudian theory. In some chapters, Horney confirmed and elucidated psychoanalytic concepts that she considered useful. For instance, she agreed with Freud that mental processes follow set rules and do not occur randomly, and that unconscious emotional motivations determine much of human behavior. But even though Horney embraced significant portions of Freud's thinking, *New Ways in Psychoanalysis* rocked the psychoanalytic community.

At least one critic accused Horney of "emptying the baby with the bath" because she coolly pointed out the defects of many pillars of psychoanalytic theory. Freud, for example, argued that the *Oedipus complex*—each child's sexual feelings for his or her parents—plays the central role in the development of a child's personality. Horney, on the other hand, asserted that the Oedipus complex is less important to emotional growth than whether or not a child feels loved. Similarly, Horney disagreed with Freud's notion that everyone is endowed with an instinctual destructiveness. Where Freud claimed that people's violent tendencies have their roots in *Thanatos*, an innate hu-

Gregory Zilboorg, one of Horney's colleagues at the New York Psychoanalytic Society, proposed that the rebel analyst be stripped of her teaching duties.

man drive toward self-destruction, she insisted that "if we want to injure or kill, we do so because we are or feel endangered, humiliated, abused."

In chapter after chapter, Horney examined Freudian concepts and laid out her own alternatives. She brought not only specific ideas but also some of the foundations of psychoanalysis into question. For instance, Freud maintained that the source of all psychological problems, which he termed *neuroses*, is an inner conflict between the drive to fulfill physical instincts and the attempt to regulate those urges. In the most revolutionary proposal made in *New Ways in Psychoanalysis*, Horney suggested instead that neuroses arise from stressful disturbances in human relationships. The most significant of these disturbances occur in childhood, she said, because they set the pattern for the *neurotic trends* of adulthood. Based on her experience with patients, Horney had concluded that an emotionally stressful childhood produces *basic anxiety*, which she defined as "a deep feeling of helplessness toward a world conceived as potentially hostile." This basic anxiety persists in adulthood, setting various neurotic trends in motion.

New Ways turned psychoanalytic theory on its head by rejecting Freud's fundamental concept that inexorable internal processes wholly determine the course of mental life. Horney accepted the importance of instinctual drives, but declared that external factors—that is, the relationships be-

During treatment sessions with the founder of psychoanalysis, the patients of Sigmund Freud lay on this couch in his Vienna office to free-associate.

tween people—play the central role in the drama of human emotion. This theory has two radical implications. Because each culture has its own distinct rules for social interaction, Horney noted, neurosis springs from different sources in different cultures. Similarly, neurosis shows itself in various ways from culture to culture because of disparities between how members of those cultures are expected to behave. In one culture, for example, a person who hallucinates might be considered insane, while in another, that person might be thought of as gifted.

The second major conclusion that Horney drew from her theory was that neurotic individuals need not, as Freud suggested, accept a life marked by perpetual inner turmoil. In her view, people have the power and the will to overcome the basic anxiety and neurotic trends that dominate their psychology—all they need in order to do so is some assistance from a trained professional. She asserted that, in attempting to guide people toward mental health, psychoanalysis should take a more "human" and less rigidly "scientific" approach than Freud recommended. According to Horney, analysts should seek "not to help the patient to gain mastery over his instincts but to lessen his anxiety to such a point that he can dispense with his 'neurotic trends.' " In order to achieve this, Horney wrote, the analyst must take a more active role in a patient's therapy. Traditional psychoanalysts often sit in near silence while their patients *free-associate*, or talk about whatever concerns them. After their patients have spoken, these analysts provide them with a technical analysis, in Freudian terms, of what their words have revealed. Horney contended that the analyst should intervene in the process of free association, asking questions and making suggestions. Analysis, she submitted, could be not only a path to self-knowledge but a source of practical advice and direction.

Thus, in *New Ways in Psychoanalysis*, Horney refuted several of the essential ideas and many of the subsidiary points of Freud's psychoanalytic theory. Her book received praise from many quarters of the medical and intellectual community, but it incited the wrath of orthodox analysts. Some of Horney's detractors accused her of misunderstanding Freud or distorting his ideas for her own purposes; others denounced as arrogant her attempt to refine his work. But Horney had observed that "the system of theories which Freud has gradually developed is so consistent that when one is once entrenched in them it is difficult to make observations unbiased by his way of thinking." Knowing this, she had not expected strict Freudians to embrace her theories without debate. Still, she had hoped her scientific colleagues would at least give her a fair hearing.

The psychoanalytic community's intolerance for divergent views distressed the freethinking Horney, who believed that even scientists who disagreed on theoretical matters could maintain friendly, constructive, professional re-

Horney's independence angered both Freud (with cigar) and his followers, who included such prominent figures as Otto Rank (top left), Ernest Jones (top right), and Sándor Ferenczi (seated, center).

lationships. But because of events occuring outside New York in 1939, many analysts resented any attempt to revise psychoanalytic theory. When *New Ways* appeared, the aging Sigmund Freud was living in London, England, having fled his Austrian homeland, which had fallen under Nazi control. There, he endured the final stages of a painful form of cancer that claimed his life in September 1939, just months after the publication of Hor-

ney's criticisms. Freud's loyal disciples charged that Horney was guilty not only of scientific heresy, but of insensitivity to the exiled, dying genius.

Following the publication of her book, Horney had found it increasingly difficult to express her views at the institute. The institute's president, Dr. Lawrence Kubie, had no tolerance for opinions that disagreed with Freud's. "There is a danger," he wrote, "of a dilution and rejection of some of the most fundamental aspects of analysis under various guises, such as progress, eclecticism, 'scientific' work, and other illusions." Like many other psychoanalysts practicing in the United States, Kubie considered it necessary to maintain the "scientific purity" of Freud's theories in order to protect psychoanalysis—just then gaining acceptance —from criticism by the scientific community at large.

In the interest of "scientific purity," Kubie kept a close watch over the instructors and students at the institute to ensure that they would not stray from Freudian principles. When students organized to propose that the institute's required curriculum be broadened and that a course taught by Horney be added, Kubie denied their request and enacted stricter guidelines for student activity. Horney continued to advise students, but those who wrote papers under her guidance were graded harshly if they revealed any interest in her theories. Students began to complain among themselves about the enforced scientific conformity of the institute.

Dr. David Levy, a former president of the New York Psychoanalytic, watched as the atmosphere at the institute deteriorated. Concerned that students' educations were suffering as a result of the disagreements among the faculty, he conducted a survey in February 1941. He asked the institute's 110 students for their opinions on academic freedom and received a disturbing response. Fully one-third of those who completed the survey said they had felt

pressured to study only those psychoanalytic viewpoints deemed acceptable by the institute's leadership. Students who had chosen to explore alternative theories reported that some faculty members tried to intimidate them into changing their course of study. Students working with unorthodox teachers such as Horney were routinely warned by other faculty members that they might not be allowed to graduate.

Levy was horrified that students at the institute no longer felt free to study whatever theories interested them. It seemed to him that the institute's administrators and its orthodox faculty

Lawrence Kubie, president of the New York Psychoanalytic, disapproved of Horney's theories. He mocked her idea of "progress" as an "illusion."

members discouraged independent thinking among teachers and students alike. Although it claimed to promote academic freedom, the institute had begun to resemble a factory designed to produce psychoanalysts in a single mold. When Levy presented his findings to Zilboorg and the Education Committee, the group listened politely and then ignored his recommendations for liberalization. The committee had its own agenda, one that did not include exposing students to the views of unorthodox scientists such as Horney.

Kubie tried to quell the growing unrest at the institute by making some small concessions to Horney and the other "liberals." In October 1939, shortly after the publication of *New Ways in Psychoanalysis*, he invited Horney to present the book's ideas to the membership of the New York Psychoanalytic, and Horney accepted. But when the meeting degenerated into a shouting match between Horney and her opponents, Kubie made no attempt to moderate the discussion or to allow Horney to explain her theory. He had obviously never had any intention of letting Horney air her views in a meaningful way.

If the October 1939 meeting frustrated Horney, the April 1941 meeting galvanized her into action. After being voted out of her post as a training analyst and walking out of the auditorium in disgust, Horney headed for a nearby bar with the four analysts who had left the meeting along with her. Their defiant act had put them in high spirits. Clara Thompson, one of the

Even before they walked out of the April 1941 meeting together, Clara Thompson (pictured) and Horney had considered forming a new analytic organization.

dissidents, later described that evening as "the most exciting thing that has happened to me in many years." The five analysts had taken a risk, they had made their statement, and now the burden of conforming to the institute's expectations slipped from their shoulders. The rebel colleagues toasted their future, which seemed full of promise. For several months Horney and Thompson had been discussing the possibility of starting a new institute. Now, the renegades decided to resign from the

New York Psychoanalytic Society and Institute and form their own psychoanalytic organization.

Horney and her friends left the bar with arms linked and marched jubilantly down Fifth Avenue. Celebrating their release from the institute, they sang a rousing spiritual, one of Horney's favorites: "Go Down Moses, / Way down in Egypt land, / Tell old Pharaoh, / to let my people go." In a sense, Horney had told "old Pharaoh"—the tyrannical psychoanalytic establishment—to let her "people"—the radical analysts—go. Finally, she was free.

Despite the difficult years that lay both behind and ahead of her, Karen Horney would succeed in leaving an indelible mark on psychoanalysis. Her new psychoanalytic institute would train young analysts in her theories, and she would continue to publish her ideas in books read not only by scientists but by people seeking solutions to their problems. The lives of hundreds of thousands of people would be touched by the work of Karen Horney.

Growing up in an unhappy household, Karen Danielsen found pleasure in schoolwork, in her friendships, and in listening "to the delicate vibrations of my soul."

TWO

"Free Thy Self from Convention"

On September 15, 1885, Clothilde Marie van Ronzelen Danielsen gave birth to a daughter, Karen Clementina Theodora Danielsen, in the town of Eilbek, Germany. A four-year-old brother, Berndt, and an assortment of other relatives welcomed Karen into the world, but no father was on hand to greet her. Berndt Henrik Wackels Danielsen, a Norwegian-born sea captain, would not meet his infant daughter until her christening two months later, when he returned from a long and dangerous ocean voyage around South America's Cape Horn.

At the time of Karen Danielsen's birth, Eilbek lay on the outskirts of Hamburg, Germany's great port city. (Later, as Hamburg expanded, the suburb became a district of the city proper.) Tall ships sailed off the North Sea into the harbor formed by the Elbe River

basin, bringing goods from around the world. Many of Eilbek's prosperous inhabitants made their living from Hamburg's lively maritime trade, and as that industry boomed during the early years of Karen's life, the little town grew. Karen and her brother, Berndt, played together in Eilbek's wooded parks and enjoyed their mother's loving attention at home in their spacious, ornately furnished apartment. They rarely saw their father, but his presence dominated the household.

Berndt Henrik Wackels Danielsen, known to everyone as Wackels, was a stern, religious man who had risen to the rank of commodore at a large commercial shipping company. Piloting ships between Europe and South America kept him at sea for six months at a time, so his children had little contact with him. Karen and Berndt liked this

Karen's mother, Sonni Danielsen, loved her children but had little in common with her religious husband. Her domineering spouse made marriage miserable for her.

arrangement, for when Wackels was home, he reigned with an iron fist. A strict Evangelical Lutheran, Wackels had no tolerance for opinions that differed from his own. As a sea captain, he was accustomed to commanding obedience—and receiving it without question. His fits of pious rage against his wife and children, during which he would often hurl his Bible at them, earned him the nickname *der Bibelschmeisser* (the Bible thrower) from the children.

Karen's mother, "Sonni," was also grateful for her husband's long absences. By marrying the 44-year-old Wackels when she was 28, she had

avoided remaining single all her life, a fate that many viewed as dreadful for women of the 19th century. Her husband's success at sea provided Sonni and her children with a comfortable living, but the marriage had made her miserable almost from the start. Sonni came from a Dutch-German family of considerably higher social rank than her husband's, and she found him unsympathetic to her cultural sophistication and liberal morality. To make matters worse, her husband's four grown children by a previous marriage never accepted her and tried to turn their father against her. Sonni took what solace she could in her own two children, but she spent much of her time ill, afflicted with depression and the various physical maladies that accompanied it.

Although terrified and resentful of Wackels much of the time, Karen loved him all the same. She admired his courage as a commander of ships on the high seas and listened eagerly to his thrilling tales of adventure in foreign lands. As a young child Karen tried everything she could to please her powerful father, but she soon realized that her handsome, charming, older brother would always be his favorite. Her own intelligence and talent meant little to a man who believed in *Kinder, Küche, Kirche* (children, kitchen, and church) as the proper spheres of feminine endeavor. Fortunately, Karen's mother did not share Wackels's philosophy. Inspired by the example of her own highly educated and fiercely independent stepmother, Sonni urged Karen to

*During Karen's youth, the great sailing ships that had long filled
Hamburg's busy harbor were replaced by modern steamships.*

pursue her ambitions, whatever they might be.

Karen Danielsen entered the local school as a kindergarten student. The progressive teaching methods employed at the *Volksschule* nourished Karen's natural curiosity, and the permissive atmosphere gave her a welcome relief from her oppressive home life. Encouraged by teachers who recognized her exceptional abilities, Karen thrived at school and earned the highest marks. She became an enthusiastic reader, devouring all kinds of books and articles. Her favorite author was Karl May, a German who wrote stories of America's wild West. Like millions of German children, Karen avidly followed the tale of Shatterhand, a young German traveling the American frontier. She particularly enjoyed reading about Winnetou, a noble Indian warrior who swears blood brotherhood with Shatterhand. Karen adopted the nickname Winnetou and, in a ritual of their own, she and her friend Gertrude ("Tutti") Ahlborn pricked their fingers and swore blood sisterhood.

By the time Karen entered the Convent School at the age of 13, her fascination with Karl May's stories had faded but her thirst for knowledge had not. She started keeping a diary that year, explaining in the very first entry that "I am enthusiastic about everything new." Karen's intellectual curiosity was stimulated at the Convent School. There, she studied German, French, history, religion, arithmetic, chemistry, and geography. She excelled in most subjects and even tutored her

friend Tutti in French. As they had in Volksschule, Karen's teachers urged her to cultivate all her academic interests. She responded enthusiastically, noting in her diary that she was "frightfully fond of going to school."

Perhaps as much as she enjoyed her studies, Karen took pleasure in the attention and support of her teachers. Not surprisingly, she developed crushes on two of them: Herr Schulze and Fräulein Banning. In her diary, Karen described Herr Schulze, her history and religion teacher, as "heavenly, i.e., interesting, clever . . . lovable, ironic, interested in us, his pupils, kindly disposed, etc." When he fell ill, Karen sent him an anonymous gift of wine; when he recovered, she gave him flowers. And when her family moved to Reinbeck, a nearby town where her beloved teacher lived, her "adoration for Herr Schulze established itself firmly." She visited him as often as she could.

As for Fräulein Banning, Karen wrote that she was "angelic, charming, interesting, clever, lovable . . . rather shy, delightful, like a sensitive plant." Karen breathlessly anticipated each meeting with her French teacher and once presented her with a birthday gift of a wooden picture frame that she had carved herself. "I'm afraid I have adored her terribly," a 15-year-old Karen reflected wistfully when her crush began to fade. As she grew older and began to look for romance, her crushes on unattainable teachers gradually lost their appeal. "Why is everything beautiful on earth given to me," she asked her diary, "only not the highest thing, not love! ... Yes, I love Mother, Berndt, Herr Schulze, Frl. Banning, etc., with all my heart. But who loves me?"

While romantic yearnings troubled Karen's heart, religious doubts troubled her soul. Wackels Danielsen saw to it that his reluctant daughter attended church regularly and entered confirmation classes when she turned 15. Nikolai von Ruckteschell, pastor of the Danielsens' church and a close friend of Karen's father, taught Wackels's harsh version of Christianity. Resistant to Ruckteschell's teaching in part because of his alliance with her strict father, Karen found confirmation lessons "horribly dull." She wrote that she "could only hate the Pastor," but she nonetheless wished she could feel some form of religious belief. "I long for the faith, firm as a rock, that makes oneself *and others* happy," she confessed to her diary. But after her confirmation Karen would write: "My day of confirmation was not a day of blessing for me. —On the contrary, it was a great piece of hypocrisy." Always ready to question ideas presented to her as absolute truth, Karen would never be able to accept institutionalized religion.

As a child, Karen enjoyed German author Karl May's tales of the American West. She took the name of her favorite character, Winnetou, as a nickname.

Frustrated in romantic and religious matters, Karen poured her energy into her studies, where she continued to flourish. She started looking toward the future and planning the course of her education and career. From the age of 13, when a kindly country doctor had treated her for the flu, Karen had dreamed of pursuing a medical career. She envisioned "years of splendid but strenuous work, then being able to serve mankind through curing diseases." But as she grew older, Karen realized she might not be able to obtain the proper training to become a doctor. Most higher education was closed to German women of the 19th century, and she faced another obstacle as well: her father's disapproval. Still, Karen knew she was not suited to the life

Dressed in a traditional German costume, 12-year-old Karen displays her doll collection.

prescribed for women of her class. She set about finding a way to get the education she wanted.

Just a few years earlier, Karen Danielsen would have found it impossible to prepare for a medical career in Germany. The few German women to obtain medical degrees before Karen's time had to leave the country to study, but fortunately for Karen the situation was about to change. The 1890s had brought an atmosphere of progress to Germany. Hamburg and other major cities had entered the industrial age. Steamboats had replaced sailing vessels, electric streetcars had replaced horse-drawn trams, and railroad lines linked cities throughout Germany.

Until 1871, the area that now makes up East and West Germany was divided into a number of culturally similar but politically independent states. But in 1870 war between France and Germany united the states in a common cause and led to their consolidation into the German Empire. In 1871 the empire adopted a constitution, which specified that the king of Prussia, Germany's largest state, serve as emperor. Kaiser Wilhelm I ascended the imperial throne on January 18, 1871. Wilhelm II, his grandson, became emperor of Germany in 1888 and pledged himself to making the German Empire a world power. German national pride, always strong, grew even stronger as citizens envisioned a glowing future for their unified country.

In the midst of Germany's transformation into a modern nation, a cry for women's rights arose. German women did not yet have the right to vote or even to participate in public meetings, and if married they were required to turn over their property and income to their husbands. Moreover, they could not attend university or even *Gymnasium*, the college-preparatory version of high school. Women's organizations began to speak out about the conditions of German women's lives. The first problem they addressed was the poor quality of the education received by most German women.

Unlike the Convent School, many schools for young women trained middle- and upper-class girls exclusively to be wives and mothers. Academic subjects often took second place

to courses in music, drawing, needlework, home economics, and conversational French, Italian, and English. Through newspaper articles and public meetings, women's rights activists convinced many Germans that women deserved the same educational opportunities as men. As a result, the level of teaching in traditional girls' schools slowly began to improve. In 1894 the first Gymnasium for girls opened in the state of Baden, followed over the next few years by several others throughout Germany. Women would finally gain entrance to German college degree programs in 1900.

When Karen heard about the opening of the Gymnasiums, she wrote, "I wanted to go right away to the Gymnasium for girls, in my thoughts I was there already." But Wackels Danielsen dashed her hopes: "My 'precious Father' forbade me any such plans once and for all," Karen wrote. She would not give up her dreams so easily, however. "He can forbid me the Gymnasium," she declared to her diary, "but the wish to study he cannot." She formulated a plan to qualify as a teacher, leave home, work, and study medicine on her own, but she soon decided to pursue another course. In December 1900 the Hamburg newspapers announced the establishment of the city's first Gymnasium courses for girls, and Karen made up her mind to attend. "I'd like to get there at Easter," she wrote, "Oh, wouldn't that be wonderful!! But Father. . . ."

Wackels Danielsen opposed Karen's attendance at the Gymnasium because he did not want to pay for an education which, he assumed, would go to waste once his daughter married. But Sonni and Berndt Danielsen stood firmly behind Karen, and both worked to persuade Wackels to pay for the classes. Berndt sought out information on the new school and told Wackels about a lecture he had heard on "the woman question," in which the speaker recommended Gymnasium educations for young women. Wackels finally agreed to allow Karen to enroll, probably only because she signed a document in which she promised to ask her father for no financial support after she graduated from Gymnasium. But even her father's stinginess could not keep Karen from exclaiming in her diary, "Oh, how happy I am!"

On April 1, 1901, Karen Danielsen enrolled at the *Realgymnasium für Jungen Mädchen* in Hamburg. Each morning she boarded the train for the half-hour ride into the city, where she reveled in the bustle of urban life and enjoyed her new status as an independent young woman. She found the first few days of classes "overwhelming, bewildering," but she was excited by the prospect of five years of serious study leading to the *Abitur*, the college entrance exam. "I am only now beginning to learn what 'learning' means," she confided to her diary. Soon, she was making new friends and immersing herself in her classes. She wrote exuberantly, "I enjoy school very much. We have to cram very hard."

Life at home remained difficult. "If only my Father were gone," Karen com-plained. But "the master of the house," as Karen referred to Wackels, did not expect to return to sea until Christmas, more than six months away. "Delightful prospect," his daughter noted dryly. Under the strain of Wackels's demands, Karen's mother fell ill and Karen herself became depressed. "I constantly have the feeling that I'm going to collapse," Karen wrote, attributing her dejection to sympathy for her mother. "Mutti [Mommy], my all, is so ill and unhappy. Oh, how I would love to help her and cheer her up. If only she had, as I do, some sort of school or other means of distraction." Not yet 16, Karen already understood how women suffered under the restrictions that society placed on them.

Just as it always had, school provided Karen with relief from family pressures. "Even though I leave home in the morning with tears in my eyes," she wrote, "I always come back cheerful." Karen excelled in her studies, but she sometimes seemed more interested in nonacademic pursuits. When she developed a crush on an actor, for instance, she started taking acting lessons from him and briefly decided to give up medicine for a career in the theater. "I will be living for art and art alone," she announced to her diary. "I'm going on the stage!!" Karen's mother opposed the plan, but this only made Karen more sure of herself. With the help of her acting teacher, Karen managed to win Sonni over. Sonni would allow Karen to study acting once she had completed enough school to qualify as a teacher.

Within a year, Karen's fantasies of a life as an actress waned. Her original ambition to practice medicine returned, now accompanied by a growing interest in psychology. When she was denied permission to attend an animal-dissection class—probably because of her sex—she decided instead to "take myself to pieces. That will probably be more difficult, but also more interesting." Karen filled the pages of her diary with minute analyses of her own emotions, motivations, and beliefs, and with reflections on the world around her. "There is such disordered turmoil in me," she wrote, "that I myself cannot burrow my way through this labyrinth. And yet: I am beginning to burrow."

Karen's awakening sexuality, and the troubling questions concerning morality that came with it, caused much of her inner turmoil. She reported that "one question occupied my mind for weeks, even months: is it wrong to give oneself to a man outside marriage or not?" Society denounced sex outside of marriage as immoral, but just as she had rejected formal religion and society's assumptions concerning women, Karen decided that conventional morality was flawed.

"A girl who gives herself to a man in free love stands morally way above the

Turn-of-the-century German feminists such as these striking textile workers strove to improve women's lives. Their success in the area of education directly benefited Karen Danielsen.

Wackels Danielsen did not believe in advanced education for women. Only after heated family debate did he allow Karen to attend Gymnasium.

woman who, for pecuniary [financial] reasons or out of a desire for a home, marries a man she does not love. . . . All our morals and morality are either 'nonsense' or immoral." Karen's words echoed those of radical 19th-century proponents of free love. Progressive thinkers of the time, such as American feminist Victoria Woodhull, protested the era's repressive attitudes toward sex and held that governments should not attempt to regulate people's sexual expression. Karen would eventually carry her skepticism regarding restrictive sexual mores into her life's work.

At the age of 18 Karen had her first real taste of the love for which she had been hoping. On Christmas Day, 1903, she met a student named Schorschi, probably one of Berndt's friends, and fell madly in love. Schorschi returned her affections, but had to return to school in another city. When he did not write for months, Karen realized that his feelings had been passing. Heartbroken, she poured out her anguish to her diary: "My walk has grown heavy and dragging and the sunny gleam in my eyes has disappeared. . . . Now death does not seem to me so terrible any more." Nonetheless, Karen could write by spring that, "I am too young, too vigorous, for this blow to break me." She began to look toward the future once more.

Almost as soon as she got over Schorschi, Karen started seeing Rolf, an impoverished music student with Bohemian (unconventional) tastes. Karen's parents disapproved of Rolf both because he would probably never make any money and because he was Jewish. Undaunted, Karen and Rolf arranged secret meetings. Rolf gradually introduced Karen to an uninhibited life of late-night cafés, where intellectuals and artists of all classes met and discussed politics, philosophy, painting, and literature. Although surprised to discover a world so different from the one in which she had grown up, Karen felt at home with the freethinking people she met and began to reexamine her values. She designed her own code of ethics, which she recorded in her diary. *"The first moral law: thou shalt not lie!* And the second: thou shalt free thyself from convention, from everyday morality, and shall think through the highest commands for thy self and act accordingly."

In August 1904, Karen's mother also decided to free herself from convention. Tormented beyond endurance by her overbearing, self-righteous husband, Sonni Danielsen left him and moved with her children to an apartment in Bahrenfeld, just outside of Hamburg. Such a move was almost unheard of in bourgeois German society, where "decent" wives stayed with their husbands no matter how they were treated. It left Sonni, Karen, and Berndt in a difficult financial position. Wackels continued to pay for the children's education, but he withheld all other support to Sonni, hoping to force her to return to him. Karen and Berndt, however, refused to let that happen, and both began tutoring other students to help support themselves and their mother.

Three weeks after Sonni left Wackels, Rolf left Karen to study music in southern Germany. Once again Karen felt desolate, and for several weeks she suffered "paralyzing fatigue and apathy." Yet, as she always had, Karen turned for comfort to her studies, to "deep absorption in the natural sciences and philosophy ... above all, therefore, hard *work*." She also continued her inner self-examination, striving "to learn how to listen to the delicate vibrations of my soul, to be incorruptibly *true to myself* and fair to others, to find in this way the right measure of my own worth." The "vibrations of the soul," the workings of the human mind, would become the focus of her life's work.

When Karen turned 20, she had already fallen in love with someone new, a young man named Ernst. "Nothing attractive about his looks," she noted in her diary, "and yet he charms me enormously." For the first time, Karen seriously contemplated marriage. She

When she started commuting to Hamburg for Gymnasium classes, Karen discovered the joys of independence. She loved to explore the city's streets and canals.

soon rejected that option, explaining that "I have a great fear that there is still a lot in me that is only waiting for the call to come forth. . . . There's something more in me." Although she longed "for a true friend, for love, for *the* man," she knew that marriage would interfere with her plans to become a doctor. She bid Ernst good-bye and turned to studying for the Abitur, the college entrance exam.

Karen was determined to be accepted at a university where she could study medicine. She plunged into preparation for the admissions test, bemoaning "that awful pressure" in her diary. "If I don't pass the exam—! Then I'm finished. Then I can't go on living," she wrote. Yet she passed the Abitur with flying colors and gained admission to Ludovico Albertina University in Freiburg im Breisgau, which offered a respected program of medical education. Karen Danielsen set off for Freiburg on Easter Sunday, 1906, to begin her medical career.

Idchen Behrman, Sonni and Karen Danielsen (standing, left to right), and Losch Grote (seated, right) relax in Freiburg, where Karen attended medical school.

THREE

"Real Work"

When Karen Danielsen arrived in Freiburg in the spring of 1906, the lively university town had a population of about 50,000. Located in the state of Baden in southwestern Germany, the city lay on the western edge of the Black Forest, 30 miles north of Switzerland and 15 miles east of France. The spires of Freiburg's great Gothic cathedral soared above the rooftops of medieval buildings dating to the 12th century, and freshwater streams ran alongside the cobbled streets. When they tired of their studies, university students could relax in the historic taverns or enjoy picnics in the forest, outings on the Rhine River, or hikes up the Schlossberg, a mountain that stood just outside town. Karen would later reminisce about Freiburg, writing, "a nameless longing steals into my heart when I think of it. . . . All the foun-

tains, the many-colored tower gates, the narrow winding streets—ah, Freiburg!"

Danielsen took a room near campus and registered for classes at Ludovico Albertina University. Founded in 1457, the school had become in 1904 the first German university to graduate women, but women still represented a tiny minority of the student body. Only 57 other women joined Danielsen at Freiburg that spring, compared with nearly 2,300 men. Many of the university's professors resented the women, and some refused to permit them in their classrooms. Some insisted that women's supposedly delicate physical and emotional consitution ruled out serious academic work and that women would ruin their health—especially their capacity for childbearing—if they studied. Others asserted that professional women were "unnatural," "un-womanly," or "masculine."

Danielsen, however, would not be discouraged. Although she occasionally wondered if she had made the right choice in deciding on a career in medicine, she never considered sacrificing her dream in order to meet society's expectations of her as a woman. Danielsen had no doubts about women's fitness or their right to pursue professional lives. She did not agree that women would stop having children if they received full educations, although she realized that few women would achieve a high degree of professional success as long as they were expected to remain "too involved with the sexual—children! etc." Nor could Danielsen accept the view of professional women as "sexual intermediate forms" or the idea that equality would adversely affect relations between the sexes. "Just compare the charming comradely relation between men and women students," she wrote, to "the unnatural formal intercourse between young people of different sex" in traditional middle-class society.

Danielsen made up her mind to prove she belonged in medical school just as much as her male colleagues did. She had no difficulty measuring up in class, but finding "comradely relations" presented more of a challenge. At first, the somewhat shy and reserved Danielsen found it hard to meet people in Freiburg. Lacking close friends, away from home for the first time, she confided to her diary that she felt "mortally unhappy to be so totally alone."

But within a few months, she met two men who would figure prominently in her life for the next several years: Louis ("Losch") Grote, a student of medicine and music, and Oskar Horney, another student visiting from out of town.

The threesome enjoyed long conversations, nights of dancing, and lazy strolls through the city and countryside. Danielsen and Grote affectionately nicknamed Horney *Hornvieh* (which translates as "horned cattle," German slang for "dimwit" or "numskull") before sending him back to Braunschweig, where he was completing work on his Ph.D. in political science. Soon, Danielsen and Grote fell in love, while Danielsen and Horney started a correspondence that would eventually become much more.

In October, at the start of the winter semester, Sonni Danielsen and Ida ("Idchen") Behrman, a Gymnasium friend of Karen Danielsen, moved to Freiburg. Behrman registered at the university, Danielsen's mother leased a large apartment, and Danielsen left her rented room to move in with her mother. To help make ends meet, the women took in two boarders: Behrman and Grote. "It is always inexpressibly cozy," Danielsen wrote to Horney of the arrangement. "We four are all so fond of one another.... One is happy when one comes home." Under the same roof, Danielsen and Grote grew closer in many ways, but "with Losch one just can't talk sense," Danielsen wrote to Horney. "I have found so few people," she added, "with whom I could have conversed about deeper-

Dominated by its impressive Gothic cathedral, historic Freiburg is nestled in the mountains of southwestern Germany. While studying there, Karen Danielsen grew fond of the city.

lying things," noting that Grote was not one of them. She relied on Horney for intellectual and spiritual sustenance, and wrote to him of her private feelings.

When Danielsen described her work to Horney, she said simply, "everything has turned to enjoyment in my hands." In her letters she recounted chemistry lectures, biology labs, and days of "intensive work" from 8:00 A.M. to 8:00 P.M. followed by "a feeling of blessed weariness." She once relayed "the happy message that we shall have a new corpse on Thursday" for dissection, which she characterized as "such real work, it gives me tremendous joy."

Still, Danielsen periodically suffered bouts of deep depression, fatigue, and *Weltschmerz*, literally "world pain," the sense that life is meaningless. These episodes worried yet intrigued the medical student, whose "ever more refined self-observation that never leaves," allowed her to describe her emotional state in detail to Horney.

Danielsen's close scrutiny of her own inner life reflected the fascination with psychology that she had developed while attending Gymnasium. This curiosity about the mind now sparked an interest in neurology, the science of the nervous system, which she began to study in school. "I have worked terri-

German medical students dissect cadavers in a 1911 anatomy class. When Karen Danielsen arrived at medical school just five years earlier, she had been one of only a few women to enroll.

Idchen Behrman, Sonni Danielsen, Losch Grote, and Karen Danielsen (left to right) shared an apartment in Freiburg. At first, Karen Danielsen termed the arrangement "inexpressibly cozy."

bly hard on the brain," she soon reported to Horney. "Now the thing begins to take shape plastically [workably] before my eyes. It was pure joy of discovery as one point after another became clear." As Danielsen found a focus for her study of medicine, the pleasure of the work gave her "something firm outside myself that I can reach out and hold to, even in my abysmally black states of mind." She wrote to Horney that "I think I would die if I should now stop studying medicine."

Danielsen's happiness in her work contrasted with a growing dissatisfaction with her personal life. She had wearied of living in close quarters with three people, including her mother, and the enforced intimacy with Grote had placed a severe strain on her relationship with him. At the same time, her correspondence with Horney was becoming increasingly flirtatious. When the two friends got together for a visit in the summer of 1907, they started a romance. Soon afterward, Horney moved to Freiburg, and for the next year he and Danielsen carried on a passionate affair. Danielsen's course work and personal life kept her so busy during her last two terms at Freiburg that she had no time to write in her diary.

In September 1908, Karen Danielsen took the *Physikum*, the examination all German medical students were required to pass before enrolling in programs of clinical training. Danielsen, who did well on the test, chose to continue her medical studies at the University of Göttingen in northern Germany. Horney planned to complete his graduate work at Göttingen as well, while Sonni decided to move to Stockholm, Sweden, to live with a stepdaughter. The little household in Freiburg broke up, and Danielsen and Horney moved north.

In Göttingen Danielsen took courses in advanced subjects such as pathology and bacteriology. She also got out of the classroom and, for the first time in her medical career, worked with actual patients in clinics. She observed experienced surgeons, obstetricians, and other specialists, then tried her own hand at healing the sick. In the clinics, Danielsen learned how to examine patients, diagnose illnesses, and provide treatment. The theories and principles she had studied in lecture halls and laboratories came to life in the clinic, and she discovered that she truly enjoyed helping people. At last, her dream of serving humanity was becoming a reality.

After a year in Göttingen, Danielsen and Horney moved to Berlin, where they married on October 31, 1909, and settled into a modest apartment. Like thousands of other young, educated Germans, the Horneys chose Berlin because of its position at the heart of the German Empire. Kaiser Wilhelm II, the emperor of Germany, lived in Berlin, the nation's capital. As the seat of Germany's government, Berlin was a thriving commercial and cultural center. Financial and manufacturing concerns expanded rapidly at the turn of the century, creating jobs that attracted workers from all over the country. Most of these laborers earned very little at their factory jobs and confronted severe housing shortages, but the city's newly rich business people could afford to spend freely on luxuries. Writers, painters, musicians, and other artists flocked to Berlin to take advantage of the city's prosperity, transforming it into one of Europe's most vital cultural communities.

Karen and Oskar Horney fit right into the bustling city of nearly 4 million. The couple's enjoyment of their new home was soon heightened by the return of Sonni Danielsen from Sweden, where she had been unhappy. Sonni moved to an apartment near the Horneys, Oskar found work at the headquarters of one of Berlin's booming industrial corporations, and Karen continued her clinical training. She registered at the University of Berlin, which at that time offered perhaps the world's finest medical education. There, she found herself in the company of students from all over Europe and the United States, who came to Berlin as

For a year after she met him in 1906, Karen Danielsen carried on a friendly correspondence with Oskar Horney. The two eventually fell in love, and they married in 1909.

much for the city's resources as for the university's. Widely considered Europe's medical capital, Berlin boasted eight major hospitals in which medical students could work.

Women made up just five percent of her medical school's student body, but this did not intimidate Horney. Ignoring the hostility expressed by some faculty members, she turned her attention to advanced courses in pharmacology, neurology, and other specialties. Horney also spent long hours at Königliche Charité hospital gaining clinical experience in such areas as surgery and pediatrics. The challenge of her studies and the satisfaction of helping the sick gave her real pleasure,

French neurologist Jean-Martin Charcot's (standing, center) use of hypnosis in the treatment of hysterical patients inspired Sigmund Freud's early psychoanalytic theory.

but Horney still suffered from bouts of nervous exhaustion. She began to seek ways to relieve her depression, and in early 1910 entered treatment with Dr. Karl Abraham, who practiced a controversial new form of therapy: psychoanalysis.

Psychoanalysis immediately captured Horney's imagination, fueling her desire to study psychiatry. This radical theory of psychology rejected some of the most basic tenets of conventional psychiatry and offered an alternative explanation of the human mind. When psychoanalysis emerged, in the late 19th and early 20th centuries, psychology was largely the domain of neurologists, one of whom defined it as "the science of the mind considered as a physical function." If psychological processes were no more than organic functions of the nervous system, neuropsychiatrists conjectured, then "abnormal" emotional conditions were manifestations of physical illness. Traumatic experiences might trigger mental problems, they said, but only if neurological weakness—usually inherited from parents—predisposed a person to psychological disturbance. Thus, the diagnosis and treatment of mental illness focused on physical factors.

Dissatisfied with neurological interpretations of psychology, Sigmund Freud, a physician from Vienna, Austria, devised a new theory, which he termed psychoanalysis. Psychoanalytic theory suggested that all psychological activity, whether healthy or unhealthy, could be explained as the interaction of conflicting mental forces. Freud asserted that every infant is born with the urge to seek physical pleasure and avoid pain. Adults inevitably interfere with this *pleasure principle*, forbidding the young child certain pleasures and requiring her or him to behave according to society's rules. Conflict then arises between the child's desire for pleasure and the desire to escape punishment for unacceptable behavior. The memory of this childhood frustration and the ongoing struggle to satisfy incompatible drives dominate the unconscious mind throughout life, providing the pattern for all psychological activity. Freud postulated that most mental activity takes place on the unconscious level and follows the set of rules defined in childhood. No psychological event occurs at random, and every psychological disturbance can be understood by analyzing its roots in the past.

Karl Abraham, Karen Horney's analyst, had studied with Freud in Vienna and brought psychoanalysis to Berlin a few years earlier. Most of the city's medical establishment, however, had greeted the new ideas coldly; as physical scientists, they viewed nonphysical interpretations of the mind with skepticism. Indeed, throughout the world Freud's theories had aroused debate which the British medical journal *Lancet* termed "more bitter than any since the days of Darwin." Like the furor over Charles Darwin's theory of evolution, first published in 1859, the controversy surrounding psychoanalysis would not die down for nearly half a century after its introduction in 1899.

45

But also like evolutionary theory, psychoanalysis would have a profound impact on western thinking of the 20th century.

Horney was among only a few students and academics who welcomed Freud's theories before World War I. She began to attend informal meetings in Abraham's home to discuss psychoanalytic theory, and resumed writing in her diary to record the progress of her own treatment. Pleased to experience the beneficial effects of the therapy for herself and to learn about psychoanalysis firsthand, Horney wrote, "undoubtedly I enjoy going to the analysis." By the end of the summer of 1910, when she finished both her analysis and her medical school course work, Horney knew that she wanted to devote her career to psychoanalysis. In preparation, she decided to specialize in psychiatry during her internship.

Horney spent the next year in preparation for her final exams while attending to a busy domestic schedule. In the fall of 1910 she discovered that she was pregnant, and in February 1911 Sonni Danielsen died. Wackels Danielsen's death the previous May had not seemed to disturb his daughter, but Horney grieved deeply for her mother. She wrote regretfully, "Had we let her feel in her lifetime all the love that has now awakened in us so powerfully, how much happier she would have been." Soon, however, the birth of Horney's first child brought new happiness. Brigitte Horney was born on March 29, 1911, and Karen Horney began to discover the pleasures and strains of motherhood, both as a woman and as a scientist. "Motherliness—perhaps that is now the focal point of my interest," she wrote in her diary. Horney would use her experience of motherhood as a basis for some of her future work in psychoanalysis.

After passing her medical exams in late 1911, Horney began a period of internship during which she was to research and write the final thesis that would qualify her for a medical doctorate degree. She spent four months at a general hospital, then transferred to Lankwitz Kuranstalt, a large psychiatric hospital. Until the end of 1912, Horney worked closely with psychiatric patients of all descriptions, deepening her knowledge of her chosen field. Her internship would offer no official training in psychoanalysis, but she pursued her controversial interest in her spare time. She completed her first analysis of a patient, writing, "Whether she'll get anything out of the analysis I don't know. I certainly will!" In 1911, Horney had joined the newly formed Berlin Psychoanalytic Society, which had grown out of Abraham's "psychoanalytic evenings." She regularly attended the society's meetings, and at one such gathering she presented a paper on the sexual education of children. Abraham reported to Freud that the paper "showed a real understanding of the material."

Horney continued her internship at a private psychiatric clinic during 1913,

While working on her doctoral thesis with Karl Bonhoeffer, who did not accept psychoanalysis, Karen Horney limited her formal studies to conventional neuropsychiatry.

leaving at the end of the year to give birth to her second daughter, Marianne. When she recovered from childbirth, she chose a sponsoring professor at the medical school and began to write her doctoral thesis. Throughout 1914 she worked for and studied with her adviser, Karl Bonhoeffer, one of the university's most respected psychiatrists. Like most of his colleagues, Bonhoeffer was not interested in psychoanalysis, so Horney had to restrict her work to more acceptable areas of psychiatry. Her final paper discussed the case of a patient suffering from *posttraumatic syndrome*, a mental disorder that results from severe emotional or physical shock. Impressed with Horney's talent as a psychiatrist, the medical school faculty granted her a medical degree. Her "real work" could begin at last.

47

This 1914 poster exhorts German women to attend a rally for woman suffrage. The position of women in German society changed rapidly in the early years of Karen Horney's career.

FOUR

"Half the Human Race"

Five months before Karen Horney received her medical degree, Germany entered World War I. The war started with the June 28, 1914, assasination of Archduke Francis Ferdinand, heir to the Austrian throne, by a Serbian nationalist (Serbia is now part of Yugoslavia). In the conflict that followed, Russia stood by its Serbian allies, thereby angering Germany, a friend of Austria. War broke out, and German battlefield casualties started pouring into Berlin from the front. From 1915 through 1918, Horney worked at Lankwitz Kuranstalt, treating soldiers who suffered from shell shock—a form of posttraumatic syndrome, the topic of her doctoral thesis—and other psychiatric disorders.

The war years presented Horney, like other German women, with new opportunity. Most of her male colleagues had been drafted and sent to the front, so Horney's services as a doctor were in great demand. And because she no longer had to worry about pleasing anti-Freudian medical school faculty, Horney could practice psychiatry as she saw fit. As soon as she received her medical degree, she began serving as an officer of the Berlin Psychoanalytic Society and applying psychoanalytic techniques to the treatment of her patients at the hospital. Her clinical success, as well as the success of others interested in analysis, began to earn psychoanalysis growing respect from the psychiatric establishment.

Oskar Horney also benefited from the war. Like many other manufacturers, his employer profited from the government's need for military equipment. As a high-ranking executive in a war-related industry, Oskar Horney was ex-

49

empt from the draft and took home a healthy share of the company's war windfall. Thus, by the middle of 1915 the Horneys could afford to buy a house of their own in the Berlin suburb of Dahlem. But despite their prosperity, the family had to make wartime sacrifices. The war disrupted agricultural production and many other functions of the German economy, and the nation focused most of its limited resources on the war effort. Civilians had to contend with rationed supplies of food, fuel, and clothing. The Horneys tightened their belts, especially after Karen Horney gave birth to Renate, her third and last daughter, in November 1916.

Horney had worked throughout her pregnancy and returned to her career soon after Renate's birth. In February 1917 she delivered her first important psychoanalytic paper, "The Technique of Psychoanalytic Therapy." Speaking before Berlin's Medical Society for Sexology, she explained the psychoanalytic process to her audience and outlined both its limitations and its potential for relieving neuroses in otherwise healthy people. In psychoanalytic sessions, patients engage in free association, telling analysts whatever crosses their mind, no matter how odd or irrelevant it might seem. Analysts interpret their patients' statements (which are filled with symbols that provide the key to patients' unconscious mind) in order to analyze the sources of patients' emotional difficulties. Over the course of treatment, patients develop mixed feelings of affection and hostility toward their analysts, reflecting the *transference* of their feelings for other people onto their analysts. With transference comes *resistance* to the therapy, when patients feel embarrassed about revealing themselves or resentful of analysts' interference in their life. When analysts have helped their patients to resolve both their transference and their resistance and to identify the causes of their psychological problems, the psychoanalysis is complete.

In her lecture, Horney asserted that the resolution of the analyst-patient relationship is more important than the analysis of what the patient says during free association. "A resistance that has been overlooked and an unrecognized transference may easily lead to failure in therapy, while an incorrect interpretation tends to correct itself," she said. Horney also explained that psychoanalysis goes beyond the treatment of specific symptoms to treat the entire psyche, or mind. In that respect, she thought, psychoanalysis represented a tremendous advance in psychiatry, which had hitherto approached mental problems as if they could be treated separately from the whole person. Horney cautioned her audience, however, against attributing the technique with magical power. Psychoanalysis, she said, "can liberate a person whose hands and feet are tied so that he may freely use his strength again, but it cannot give him new arms and legs."

This lecture marked Horney's emergence as a full-fledged psychoanalyst who now devoted all of her scientific

German soldiers march to the front during World War I. Germany's humiliating, costly defeat in that conflict caused severe social and political upheaval in Horney's native country.

energy to Freudian theory. Shortly afterward, the Horneys purchased a large home in Zehlendorf, an affluent Berlin suburb. There, on three acres of their own, they found refuge from the political unrest sweeping the city. World War I had worn down the German people, and it had become obvious to everyone that Germany was on the verge of losing the conflict. Those at home were weary of the deprivation they had endured; those returning from the front were disgusted that so much blood had been shed in vain. Seeking someone to blame for their country's imminent defeat, German citizens lashed out at Kaiser Wilhelm II and his court. Sporadic strikes and street violence plagued Berlin for most of 1918, and in November the kaiser was finally

Horney picnics with daughters Brigitte (left) and Marianne (right). She planned to give her daughters a "good psychoanalytic upbringing."

forced to abdicate his throne and flee the country.

Once the imperial government was overthrown, several political groups began to vie for control of the country. Demonstrations erupted into bloody street battles as the Spartacists, a communist group led by Rosa Luxemburg, struggled with the moderate Social Democrats and various right-wing forces. In January 1919, Germans elected a provisional government, giving the Social Democrats the upper hand in the new national assembly. Meeting in the city of Weimar, the assembly drew up a constitution for a representative democracy, and in February it declared the birth of the Weimar Republic. That May, the new government signed the Treaty of Versailles, officially admitting Germany's defeat and ending World War I.

Karen Horney opened her first private practice after peace was declared. She saw patients both at her suburban home and in the office she had set up in Berlin. Because most of Horney's patients were women, the analyst was able to immerse herself in an exploration of feminine psychology. As a woman, a mother, and, most important, as a scientist, Horney found the female psyche of immense interest. She spent more and more of her time examining women's emotional lives from the perspective of psychoanalysis and soon came to the conclusion that Freudian theory fell woefully short in its attempts to describe feminine psychology. She set out to reform the psychoanalytic view of women.

At the same time, Horney kept very busy in the Berlin psychoanalytic community. She gave up her post as secretary of the Berlin Psychoanalytic Society but remained active in the group, which recognized her as one of its foremost members. When the Berlin Society decided to open a clinic, Horney was one of its six founding members and its only woman director. In February 1920, the Poliklinik opened its doors, offering treatment for the poor, training for young analysts, and an atmosphere that encouraged experienced analysts to conduct original research.

Maintaining her private practice on a part-time basis, Horney also treated patients and taught students at the Poliklinik. Along with senior training analyst Hanns Sachs, her friend Karl Muller-Braunschweig, and others, Horney set up a committee to design a standardized training program for would-be analysts. Over the next few years, the committee devised formal requirements for candidates. Each had to undergo an approved training analysis, attend a designated number of lectures, and present one formal paper before being approved as a psychoanalyst. Horney later published the committee's guidelines in a paper entitled "The Establishment of a Training Program: On Its Organization." The program described in the paper remains the standard format for psychoanalytic training today.

Quickly establishing an international reputation, the Poliklinik drew increasing numbers of analysts and candidates from all over the world. It also attracted growing attention from the world's medical and intellectual

Rosa Luxemburg (in checked skirt) led German Communists in their 1918 effort to incite a proletarian revolution. She was murdered in 1919 by right-wing forces.

communities. Berlin soon replaced Vienna, the home of Sigmund Freud, as the center of the psychoanalytic movement. The International Psychoanalytic Association chose the city as the site for its 1922 congress, to be chaired by Freud. That fall, more than 250 analysts, including Horney, gathered to present their work and discuss the future of psychoanalysis. Horney delivered a paper to her colleagues, the topic of which foreshadowed the course her work would take over the next 13 years.

"On the Genesis of the Castration Complex in Women" addresses Freud's theory of female sexuality. Viewing sexuality as central to human psychology, Freud made it a focal point of psychoanalysis. His theory divided sexual development into four stages. During the first stage, termed *infantile sexuality*, children up to the age of seven or so experience certain physical desires that Freud identified as sexual. Children in this stage of development attempt to fulfill their drives through various means. From about the age of 7 through 12, however, children suppress these urges and pass through a period of *latency*. Finally, in *puberty*, which encompasses the next few years, children rediscover their sexuality and establish the patterns of sexual behavior that will characterize their adult life. Once puberty is complete, the *genital phase*, that of mature adult sexuality, begins.

Freud, who regarded the period of infantile sexuality as the most important stage of human sexual development, broke it down into three phases. He theorized that, up to the age of approximately one and a half, infants find primary sexual satisfaction in eating, sucking, and other oral activities. The next year and a half centers around the anus, as children derive their greatest enjoyment from defecation. Then, starting at about age three, children enter what Freud termed the *phallic stage*, during which their genitals serve as the center of physical pleasure. At this point, female sexual development diverges from that of the male, just as Horney's view of sexuality begins to differ from Freud's.

During the phallic stage, according to Freud, girls and boys notice the differences in their genitalia. Girls come to the conclusion that their lack of a penis is a "defect" and develop *penis envy*, the desire to have a penis of their own. The young girl believes that, although she once had a penis, she lost it as punishment for some misbehavior and was left with a "wound"—her vagina—as "proof" of her castration. This *castration complex*, Freud believed, shows up in women as feelings of inferiority to and bitterness toward men. Based on her experiences as a practicing analyst, Horney found the assumption "that females feel at a disadvantage because of their genital organs" unacceptable. She wrote that male analysts might not have considered the notion problematic, "possibly because to masculine narcissism [egoism] this has seemed too self-evident to need explanation."

The "assertion that one half of the human race is discontented with the sex assigned to it . . . is decidedly unsatisfying, not only to feminine narcissism but also to biological science," Horney continued. She did not deny that young girls experience penis envy, but she assigned it only a minor role in female psychology. Horney also agreed with Freud that women suffer lifelong feelings of rage and envy toward men, but argued that these feelings do not arise from penis envy. Instead, Horney asserted, the castration complex springs from the disappointment felt by girls when their sexual fantasies involving their father are not fulfilled.

Freudian theory holds that young boys and girls have unconscious sexual urges concerning their parents. Their urges are usually frustrated because of the almost universal taboo against incest. Freud termed this the Oedipus complex after Oedipus, a figure in Greek legend who unknowingly killed his father and married his mother. Horney theorized that, when girls feel physical desire for their father and are denied fulfillment, they feel betrayed by and angry toward their father. Hurt,

Freud (second row, center) and his followers gather for an early psychoanalytic congress. From the start, women were a significant force in the movement.

An early 20th-century poster protests restrictive German abortion laws. In her own work, Horney decried cultural strictures on the free expression of female sexuality.

they decide that the feminine role is less desirable than the male role. They then seek to emulate their father, whose gender brings with it numerous social and sexual privileges. Thus, resentment of their father—and by extension, of all men—and a desire to enjoy male advantages, generates the castration complex in women.

Horney's paper was well received at the congress, in part because it did not deviate too far from accepted Freudian doctrine. Still, it established her as an independent thinker and an expert on feminine psychology. Unfortunately, Horney's success was soon followed by grief. Early in 1923 her brother, Berndt Danielsen, died at the age of 41. Crushed, Horney wrote that his death was "totally senseless," but she continued her work, taking solace in the activity. When the thriving Poliklinik was renamed the Psychoanalytic Institute of the Berlin Society a few months later, Horney was put in charge of the training program, its primary function. The ongoing vitality of the institute, however, did not mirror the political and economic situation in Berlin or in Germany as a whole, nor did Horney's professional well-being reflect the condition of her marriage.

Burdened with war debt and food shortages, the German economy had weakened progressively since World War I. Unemployment had risen steadily, leaving millions out of work. Runaway inflation crippled the country, so that by the end of 1923, 1 billion deutsche marks bought what 1 mark had bought in 1914, and 4 trillion marks bought just 1 U.S. dollar. Workers were paid as often as twice a day and spent their money immediately, knowing that it would be worth much less within hours. Finally, the German bank system collapsed, and with it, Oskar Horney's investments. Oskar Horney fell seriously ill shortly after he discovered that he was bankrupt. When he finally recovered eight months later, he remained morose, defeated, and withdrawn. The strain took its toll on the Horneys' marriage, and Oskar and Karen drifted slowly apart.

The Horneys' marital difficulties were nothing new: Although they liked each other well enough, the couple's initial passion had long since cooled. Each was deeply involved in a career that held little interest for the other. Their children, now aged 13, 11, and 8, served as one of the only bonds between Oskar and Karen Horney, but even that was a weak link. Neither Oskar, a typical father of his era, nor Karen, a busy scientist, had much time for the girls. Brigitte, Marianne, and Renate spent most of the year away at boarding school or at home under the care of a governess. Their independence pleased Karen Horney, who spoke of her approach to child rearing as a "good psychoanalytic upbringing."

Horney recognized the limitations of such an upbringing only after she decided to have her daughters analyzed. She sent the girls to pioneering child analyst Melanie Klein, a brilliant and controversial theorist, but Klein had

This 1923 Käthe Kollwitz drawing, The Survivors, *depicts victims of Germany's post–World War I economic breakdown. The country's 1923 bank collapse ruined Oskar Horney.*

not yet perfected her technique. Horney's daughters found analysis an unpleasant, fruitless task and soon persuaded their mother to call it off.

This disappointment, though, did not shake Karen Horney's faith in psychoanalysis. She continued to treat patients, train students, and lecture frequently, inspiring admiration on all sides. One student, quoted in Jack Ru-

bin's biography *Karen Horney: Gentle Rebel of Psychoanalysis*, recalled Horney as "an impressive and beautiful woman towards whom one developed an almost immediate deep confidence." Horney also reached out beyond the psychoanalytic community, often addressing audiences unfamiliar with analysis. Listeners responded enthusiastically to her clear, direct descriptions of psychoanalytic theory. Horney's talent for explaining complex concepts in simple language would remain a hallmark of her career.

Despite Horney's success as an analyst, she and her husband had to sell their house at the end of 1925. The government had managed to stabilize the German economy, but Oskar Horney was finished in business and the family had debts to pay. The Horneys moved into a large apartment in the center of Berlin, but early in 1926 they decided to separate. Karen Horney and her three daughters moved to a smaller, more affordable flat where, for the next couple of years, they would struggle to make ends meet. Depressed over the failure of her marriage and worried about the uncertainty of the future, Horney nonetheless felt as if she had shed a heavy load. At the age of 40, she prepared for one of the most productive and rewarding periods of her career.

A German woman lights her stove with several million deutsche marks. In the years following World War I, skyrocketing inflation made German currency almost worthless.

During the late 1920s and early 1930s Karen Horney formulated a psychoanalytic theory of feminine psychology. Her work refuted Freudian theory and angered conservative analysts.

FIVE

Departures

Unlike the breakup of her parents' marriage nearly 22 years earlier, Karen Horney's separation from her husband in 1926 was not considered scandalous. Times had changed in Germany, especially in cosmopolitan Berlin, and women now enjoyed educational, professional, and personal independence unlike any they had known before. This advance had come largely as the result of World War I, which had not only brought about political and economic upheaval but had thrown German society into a state of flux. Defeated and disillusioned, previously conservative citizens questioned their traditional values, and many Berliners cast off their old morality altogether. They viewed long-established institutions such as religion, marriage, and the law with skepticism, and they embraced individual freedom as their ideal. Many experimented with free love and open marriage and eagerly welcomed new social and cultural movements.

Berlin's artists and intellectuals flourished in this progressive atmosphere. In Berlin, physicist Albert Einstein formulated the theory of relativity; artists George Grosz, Tristan Tzara, and their fellow dadaists outraged the art world with their defiant work; filmmaker Fritz Lang revolutionized cinema; and playwright Bertolt Brecht redefined German theater. Meanwhile, Berliners celebrated the work of architects Walter Gropius and Mies van der Rohe, painters Wassily Kandinsky and Paul Klee, and other members of the Bauhaus design movement. Kandinsky and Klee, along with Max Beckman and many lesser-known artists, also brought German Expressionist painting to its peak during the 1920s. Expressionism, an intensely emotional, highly personal vision of the world, dominated German literature, theater, and film as well, yielding such masterpieces as the great silent film *The Cabinet of Doctor Caligari*.

As members of psychology's avant-garde, psychoanalysts found Berlin a hospitable place to live and practice. Karen Horney, a nonconformist even when compared with her colleagues, thrived in the stimulating urban milieu. Freed now from marital constraints, she frequently spent her evenings in cafés, debating psychoanalysis, politics, and philosophy with her students and friends. Among those she met in the cafés were psychoanalytic student Erich Fromm; Erich Maria Remarque, author of *All Quiet on the Western Front*; and Protestant theologian Paul Tillich. Tillich's views on the relationship between religion, psychoanalysis, socialism, and existentialism would later have a profound impact on Horney's theories of psychoanalysis.

In the 6 years between her separation from Oskar Horney and her emigration from Germany, Karen Horney published 17 psychoanalytic papers, 13 of them on the topics of feminine psychology or marriage. In these papers, she became increasingly critical of Freud and moved steadily away from orthodox analysis. Horney's extensive work with patients had convinced her that Freudian theory, particularly where it concerned women, was seriously flawed in at least two significant ways: It granted too much importance to penis envy, and too little to the effect of social factors on psychological development.

The psychoanalytic emphasis on the penis as the focus of both male and female sexuality arose from the discipline's male bias, according to Horney. "Psychoanalysis is the creation of a male genius," Horney noted in a 1926 paper, "and almost all those who have developed his ideas have been men." Because of this, she wrote, "the psychology of women has hitherto been considered only from the point of view of men." Horney remarked that male-oriented psychoanalytic theory reflected culture as a whole, in that it equated "human being" with "man" and assumed the masculine perspective represented objective truth. "Our whole civilization is a masculine civilization," she wrote, noting that such a culture requires women to comply with restrictive, male-defined social principles.

As participants in a "masculine civilization," Freudians assumed that women's minds and emotions were ruled by the same phallic consciousness that they believed dominated male psychology. Horney's extensive work with female patients, however, had led her to disagree with the Freudian assertion that the lack of a penis was the most significant force governing feminine psychology. Instead, she granted female physiology and a positive awareness of femininity the same importance for girls that the presence of male genitalia and a masculine identity had for boys.

Freud asserted that young girls envy boys their penises because they feel deprived of what he termed in a 1933 lecture "the boy's far superior equipment." Horney, by contrast, believed that the *primary penis envy* felt by young girls springs not from a sense of inferiority to boys but from three simple physical factors. Young girls envy boys, she said, because boys can more easily see and touch their own genitals and can urinate standing up. Horney

A scene from Fritz Lang's 1932 film M *typifies expressionistic German cinema between the wars. Such films often used disturbing imagery to explore psychological themes.*

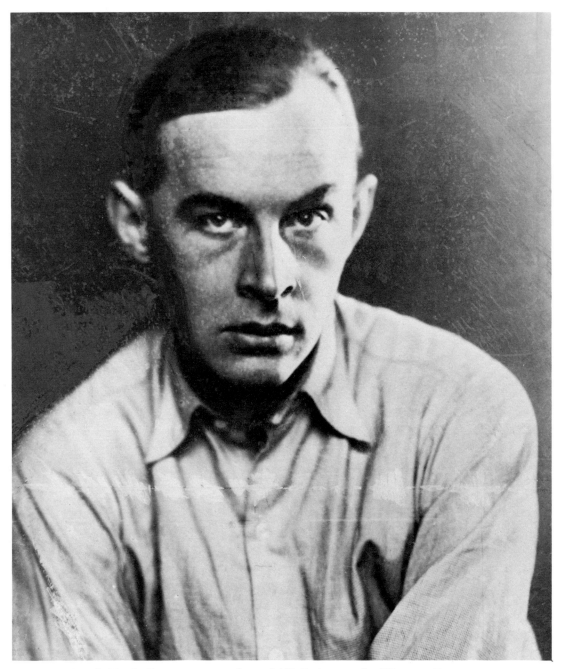

Erich Maria Remarque, author of All Quiet on the Western Front, *numbered among Horney's friends in Berlin. The two remained close after both immigrated to the United States.*

had determined, however, that this primary penis envy soon fades and thus does not determine the course of further female sexual development.

Of course, Horney recognized that many girls do feel a complex of emotions that she referred to as *secondary penis envy*. But contrary to Freud's theory, this envy—revealed as a wish to take on the male role—has its basis in the real experiences of early childhood. As Horney had described in her 1923 paper, girls' Oedipal fantasies concerning their fathers produce a desire to be like their fathers. Horney now defined this as secondary penis envy and asserted that it is "reinforced and supported by the actual disadvantage under which women labor in social life." Since society teaches girls from birth that they are inferior to boys, "the girl carries with her a reason for envy of the male ... this social impression must contribute to justify her masculinity wishes on a conscious level, and ... impedes an inner affirmation of her female role."

Despite the difficulties of being a woman in a man's world, Horney wrote, few women truly wish to be men. In her view, which stood in direct opposition to Freud's, women's enjoyment of their femininity plays at least as great a role in their emotional life as do any envious or resentful emotions they might harbor concerning men. When women do experience sexual or emotional dissatisfaction, it is not usually rooted in a deep-seated desire to be male. Instead, said Horney, such dissatisfaction arises in response to cultural forces that "work to restrict woman in the free unfolding of her femininity." Devalued and confined by "masculine civilization," women must struggle to acquire and retain any good feelings about themselves and their sexuality.

Freud, on the other hand, maintained that women can find true sexual fulfillment only in pregnancy and childbirth. Children, he said, serve as a substitute for the penis a woman can never have. Horney disputed this. Childbearing, she stated, is not merely a consolation for the "misfortune" of being born female. Rather, it is a uniquely and entirely feminine experience, a rich expression of womanhood completely removed from the issue of penis envy. Horney was astounded that Freud could reduce "the blissful consciousness of bearing new life ... the deep pleasurable satisfaction in suckling ... and the happiness of the whole period" of infancy to the imagined fulfillment of a desire for a penis.

Horney soon devised a theory to explain why Freud slighted motherhood. She had received, in her work with male patients, "a most surprising impression of the intensity of [their] envy of pregnancy, childbirth, and motherhood" and had found that this "womb envy" has several implications. Some of these are positive, such as men's tendency to transform their wish to bear children into creative activity. But male envy of women's reproductive capabilities has a negative effect on relations between the sexes. Because men cannot experience the motherhood they desire, Horney wrote, they

65

disdain it as "a burden, and . . . may be glad that they have not to bear it."

Male depreciation of female sexual functions, Horney asserted, broadens into a generalized contempt for women, a cultural notion that woman is "a second-rate being . . . prevented from real accomplishment by the deplorable, bloody tragedies of menstruation and childbirth." Viewing women as objects of pity, "every man silently thanks his God . . . that he was not created a woman," she wrote. Horney considered Freud's theory of feminine psychology a sophisticated version of that prayer.

Freud himself had admitted that psychoanalysis as yet presented an incomplete picture of the female psyche, but he did so grudgingly. "We have only described women in so far as their natures are determined by their sexual function," he conceded, adding reluc-

Benefiting from early 20th-century advances in education for women, female students attend a gym class. The Nazis hoped to reverse the progress made by German feminists.

tantly that, "an individual woman may be a human being apart from this." Although he knew that more work remained to be done in the area of feminine psychology, Freud did not take kindly to the attempts of Horney—and others who disagreed with him—to refine his theories. In 1925, even before Horney had formulated her most forceful arguments against him, Freud dismissed work such as hers as the efforts of "feminists, who are anxious to force us to regard the two sexes as equal in position and worth." He suggested in 1931, after reading papers by Horney and analysts sympathetic to her theories, that it was "quite natural that the female sex should refuse to accept a view which appears to contradict their eagerly coveted equality with men." Freud rejected as worthless any psychoanalytic work that treated men and women as "equal in position and worth."

Taking their lead from Freud, many of Horney's peers grew decidedly cooler toward her. The majority of the analytic community still viewed Freud with unquestioning reverence and could not tolerate criticisms of his work. Although Horney had earned respect as an experienced and highly talented analyst and had served as secretary-treasurer of the Berlin Psychoanalytic Society throughout the late 1920s, her reputation suffered as a result of Freud's disapproval. Horney's conservative colleagues increasingly saw her as a troublemaker and began to distance themselves from her. Finally,

Social Democrats waged a bitter campaign against the Nazis in Germany's 1930 election, using sensationalistic posters such as these. The Nazis, however, won 100 Reichstag seats.

in January 1931, Horney resigned her official post. She was not, however, the only analyst to run up against these difficulties. A few other dissenters, some of them Horney's friends, had already left Berlin in search of professional freedom. The destination of choice was America.

Berlin's golden years were drawing to a close. As the United States and Eu-

Lionel Blitzsten was a cofounder of the Institute for Psychoanalysis in Chicago. Like Horney, he disagreed with Franz Alexander on many psychoanalytic points.

rope plunged into the Great Depression, Germany's fragile economy—and with it, Berlin's artificial prosperity—collapsed. Skyrocketing unemployment aggravated the nation's political distress, as many Germans blamed their economic woes on the Social Democrats who dominated the government. The disgruntled populace began to lend greater support to two other parties: the Communists and the National Socialists, better known as the Nazis. Communism, an ideology centered around the elimination of private property, eco-

nomic inequity, and organized government, stood in direct opposition to nazism. The Nazis espoused racism, sexism, anti-Semitism, militarism, and fascism, a philosophy of fanatical nationalism and rigid state control over all aspects of life.

The Nazi promise to bring law and order to Germany appealed to many who had wearied of the nation's political, economic, and social turmoil. From a nationwide total of 26,000 in 1926, Nazi party membership rose to 400,000 in 1931. The Nazis won 6.5 million votes and 100 Reichstag seats in the September 1930 election, establishing the party as a major political force. As they gained support, the Nazis gained confidence and attempted to suppress their opposition, especially in Berlin. Encountering strong resistance from Berliners, who favored the Social Democrats and the Communists, Nazis took to the city's streets and used violence against their enemies.

Faced with the rapid deterioration of life in Germany as well as with the disapproval of most of her colleagues, Karen Horney looked toward the West. Psychoanalysis was gaining a foothold in America, and some of her former Berlin peers were already working to establish training programs there. One of them, Franz Alexander, had gone to Chicago to found the Institute for Psychoanalysis. In mid-1931 he telephoned Horney and invited her to join him and help set up the program. She accepted his offer of a position as assistant director and arranged to start her new job the following year.

Chicago was a booming urban center when Horney arrived in 1932. In some ways it reminded her of Berlin, which one writer dubbed the "European Chicago."

Horney spent the next several months preparing to leave Germany— and two of her daughters. Brigitte, now 21, had embarked on a promising acting career and wished to stay in Germany to pursue it. Eighteen-year-old Marianne was studying medicine at the University of Freiburg and intended to finish her work there before leaving for America, where she planned to con-

clude her training. The only one of Horney's children to travel with her would be Renate, a student of 15. Bidding good-bye to their friends, family, and homeland, the two Horney women set out for a new world in August 1932.

When Karen and Renate Horney arrived in Chicago, the prosperity and bustle of the growing city reminded them of Berlin in the 1920s. But where

Horney (center) enjoys a ride in the Illinois countryside with colleague Leon Saul (left) and her daughter Renate. The analyst adapted easily to life in America.

Berlin had been an old European city of culture, Chicago was a raw young city of commerce which, even in the depths of the Great Depression, had a brash image. The 18th Amendment to the Constitution, outlawing the sale of alcoholic beverages in the United States, had turned the midwestern city into a headquarters for violent bootleggers and gangsters who fought for control of the black market in liquor. The Horneys, in fact, got a glimpse of the underworld on their first night in Chicago, when they witnessed a robbery and shoot-out in the lobby of their hotel.

Hoping to settle into a more normal routine, Horney rented an apartment near the psychoanalytic institute, on the city's North Side. Renate enrolled in a progressive school while her mother took up her professional duties. As one of a staff of seven, Horney conducted training analyses of students, supervised their work with patients, and taught several courses on psychoanalytic technique and feminine psychology. Her students and colleagues regarded her with deep respect, both for her European training and for her talent as a teacher and theorist.

Nonetheless, Horney received no special treatment from the Illinois State Medical Board. She had to study for months and pass an exam in English before she qualified to practice medicine in the United States. Establishing her American medical credentials not only enabled Horney to practice her profession, it also aided her attempts to win support for analysis from the medical and lay communities. Toward this end, Horney and the other senior analysts at the institute delivered scores of lectures to nonanalytic audiences.

In the course of this work, Horney met many prominent intellectuals from outside the medical community, including anthropologist Margaret Mead. Mead's studies of the effects of cultural influences on human behavior paralleled Horney's own work. Horney found anthropology fascinating and useful and increasingly took cultural factors into account in her theories of psychology. Another prominent figure in Horney's circle was social philosopher Erich Fromm, whom she had first met in Berlin when he was studying psychoanalysis at the Poliklinik. Horney found Fromm's theories of how people adapt to their societies very interesting. As a philosopher and psychoanalyst, Fromm used Freudian theory to analyze social problems. He and Horney, who took social issues into account when formulating psychoanalytic theory, developed a particularly fruitful working relationship. They would remain close friends for years to come.

Horney's career prospered along with the fortunes of the Institute for Psychoanalysis. As she hit her stride professionally Horney adjusted to American life and found that she liked it a great deal. In January 1933, the same month that Nazi leader Adolf Hitler became chancellor of Germany, Horney went to the district courthouse in Chicago and filed a "declaration of intention" to become an American citizen. She learned to enjoy the casual freedom of her chosen land and began to set aside her European modesty and reserve. Margaret Mead, who had at first described Horney as a "'typical' Viennese intellectual . . . [with] a studiously neglected appearance," soon noted that the analyst "looked elegant, with an expensive hat and dress."

Now firmly established in America, Karen Horney returned her full attention to psychoanalysis. She presented her first important American paper, "The Problem of Feminine Masochism," at a Washington, D.C., meeting of the American Psychoanalytic Association (APA). Again addressing Freud's theory of feminine psychology, Horney refuted his notion that women are intrinsically masochistic, that is, that they naturally enjoy being dominated and even abused. Horney's clinical experience had shown that women generally adopt the submissive role not because of biological inclination but because of "certain fixed ideologies concerning the 'nature' of woman; that she is innately weak, emotional, enjoys dependence, is limited in capacities for independent work and autonomous thinking. It is obvious that these ideologies function not only to reconcile women to their subordinate role, but also to plant the belief that it represents a fulfillment they crave, or an ideal for which it is desirable to strive."

Clearly, Horney herself had a great capacity for autonomous thinking, and

Embroiled in disputes with Franz Alexander after less than two years in Chicago, Horney decided to move to New York City to practice psychoanalysis.

once again her scientific independence began to cause problems. She had already come into conflict with Franz Alexander over a number of issues, including the institute's approach to psychoanalytic training. Where Alexander took a more orthodox view of the issues, Horney often favored experimentation with new techniques. Their disagreement mirrored a rift that had developed in the American psychoanalytic community between Freudian purists and revisionists. Publication of Horney's increasingly controversial work placed her squarely in the revisionist camp, thus increasing tensions between herself and the conservative Alexander. But analysts on the East Coast had given her work a warm reception. Horney had lectured frequently at the Washington-Baltimore Psychoanalytic Society and Institute and at the New York Psychoanalytic Society and Institute, and she had developed strong ties to the two organizations. When her contract with the Institute for Psychoanalysis ran out in September 1934, Horney decided to move to New York and open a private practice.

In New York City, Karen Horney continued to stir up psychoanalytic controversy. Her theories departed ever more radically from Freud's, alienating her orthodox colleagues.

SIX

Taking a Stand

When Karen Horney arrived in New York City she was 49 years old. A prominent figure in intellectual and scientific circles, she nonetheless had an ambiguous image. On the one hand, her peers respected her impeccable European training and experience; on the other, many ignored or scoffed at her attempts to refine Freudian theory. Summarizing the opinion of the maverick analyst held by many conservative Freudians, Franz Alexander wrote, "She had excellent critical faculties, but did not succeed in supplying anything substantially new and valid for what she tried to destroy." Although Horney was admired as a brilliant teacher and therapist, she had yet to earn the regard of her colleagues as a great researcher and theorist. This did not discourage her; she seemed, in fact, hardly aware of it as she set out to make a new life in New York. She had work to do, and could not waste time worrying about the opinions of others.

In the summer of 1933, Marianne Horney had arrived in Chicago to complete her medical training. She and Renate remained in Chicago when their mother left, Marianne to finish medical school and Renate to attend college. Brigitte still lived and worked in Berlin, where the German film industry thrived. Alone for the first time in a quarter century, Horney looked forward to uninterrupted days of work. She took an apartment near Central Park, choosing a hotel in which maid service freed her from most household duties. She then opened an office on the Upper East Side of Manhattan and soon had a full roster of patients. Even in the depths of the Great Depression, so many wealthy patients wanted treatment from the esteemed Dr. Horney that the analyst had to turn quite a few away. Her practice afforded her a comfortable living, but she had no intention of settling down to a quiet routine.

Horney joined the New York Psychoanalytic Institute and there began teaching a series of courses in clinical technique. She also continued to publish scholarly papers, and she volunteered her psychiatric services to the United Jewish Aid Society (later called the Jewish Family Service). The society helped Jewish refugees from Europe adjust to life in the United States. Throughout the late 1930s, German and Austrian Jews flooded into America to escape the harshly anti-Jewish rule of the Nazis. Horney, as a specialist in psychology, gave advice to the Jewish Aid social workers who provided assistance to the refugees. She also worked with some of the refugees herself, helping them cope with the wrenching changes they faced. The director of the program later recalled that Horney "seemed so down to earth, able to meet patients on their level. They felt at home with her and peaceful. She was dynamic and full of life."

New York itself was becoming more dynamic and full of life as refugees poured into the city. Not only did Jews of all descriptions flee the Nazis in the years preceding World War II, but hundreds of scientists, philosophers, painters, and writers (many of whom also happened to be Jewish) left their Nazi-dominated homelands as well. As the Nazis took control of academic, scientific, and cultural institutions, they imposed restrictions on creative activity. Only work that conformed to Nazi ideology was officially tolerated, so intellectuals and artists no longer enjoyed the freedom to work honestly, unimpeded by political concerns. Instead, they were required to promote the racist, militaristic ideals of the Nazis. Many fled rather than compromise their beliefs and cooperate with the Nazis. Others left because they foresaw dark days ahead for Europe.

New York City soon supported a large German-speaking intellectual community, much of whose activity centered around the New School for Social Research. The New School, a progressive Downtown institution dedicated to advanced adult education, had expanded in response to the influx of European scholars into the United States. Under a program known as the University in Exile (now called the Graduate Faculty), the New School hired scores of the new immigrants as teachers and lecturers. Soon boasting an impressive faculty that included psychoanalyst Alfred Adler and political philosopher Hannah Arendt, the school became one of the country's most vibrant centers of learning during the 1930s and 1940s. One faculty member described it as "a place of constant experimentation and of complete freedom for teachers and students."

The atmosphere of the New School appealed to Horney. In the fall of 1935 she began teaching a New School course, the first of many she would offer at the institution over the next 17 years. Entitled "Culture and Neurosis," her first lecture series dealt with an issue that had replaced feminine psychology as Horney's primary theoretical concern. Horney had come to view the psychological development of individuals as a product of cultural influences. This set her in direct opposition to Freud and other orthodox analysts, who held that fundamental human instincts determined the character of people's emotional lives.

Horney's course reflected the new direction that her work had taken under the influence of Erich Fromm, Paul Tillich, Margaret Mead, and cultural anthropologist Ruth Benedict. Horney's affiliation with the New School gave her the opportunity to refine her theories of social psychology even further. At the school she participated in seminars on the relation of sociology and psychology, the issue that would claim most of her professional attention in the years to come.

Nazis burn books at the University of Berlin in 1933. Cultural oppression prompted many intellectuals and artists to flee Germany before World War II.

Horney's lectures proved wildly popular with students at the New School. The analyst's ability to communicate complex psychoanalytic concepts in clear, simple language allowed her listeners to understand the previously mysterious discipline and to see why and how it was making such a profound impact on Western thought. The lectures drew their power not only from Horney's ability as a teacher, but from the contents of her talks. Unlike typical psychoanalytic lecturers, Horney presented abstract concepts in the context of discussions of real people and their problems. Listening to her, audience members could easily draw connections between analytic theory and their own life. Horney's New School lectures were always packed.

Walter Norton, head of a large Manhattan publishing company, immediately recognized Horney's unique talent and asked her to turn her lecture series into a book. Eager to bring psychoanalysis to the widest possible audience, she quickly agreed to write the book. She made room in her already hectic schedule of teaching, counseling, and volunteering and set about organizing her ideas for publication.

Even in the midst of so much professional activity, Horney found time for a rich social life. She made dozens of new friends in the intellectual community and renewed her personal relationships with Fromm, recently transplanted from Chicago, and with Paul and Hannah Tillich, newly arrived from Germany. Horney grew especially close to Hannah Tillich, who treasured Hor-

Austrian psychiatrist Alfred Adler, a former Freud associate who had rejected psychoanalysis, was a prominent figure at the New School's University in Exile.

ney's "beautiful, but invisible, attention." As the wife of a famous man, Tillich admired Horney's particular sensitivity to women. She once remarked that, even in the company of the most brilliant men, Horney would "never forget the woman." Horney's circle of friends gave countless dinner and cocktail parties and sometimes vacationed together on Monhegan Island, Maine, or in the Hamptons on Long Island, New York. Hannah Tillich fondly recalled the "wonderful festive European style" that Horney brought to these activities.

European style of another sort came rapidly to the New York Psychoanalytic Institute in the late 1930s. Until now, Germany and Austria had served as the capitals of the psychoanalytic world, but with the rise of the Nazis, most analysts had decided to emigrate. Among the many cultural movements that the Nazis tried to suppress was psychoanalysis, of which they were especially critical. They threatened its practitioners with punishment if they refused to water down their views on psychology. Not only was analysis the "corrupt" creation of a Jew, it focused on sexuality as the key to the human psyche. The Nazis, who embraced a rigidly straitlaced view of sexual morality, misinterpreted Freud's candid treatment of sexuality and condemned his theories as perverse. For similar reasons, they banned jazz—which they considered sexually provocative—and sent homosexuals to concentration camps along with Jews, gypsies, Communists, and other "undesirables."

Forbidden to practice their profession in Germany, many of the world's foremost psychoanalysts chose the United States, most frequently New York, as their new home. The New York Psychoanalytic Institute expanded rapidly. With the arrival of influential European analysts, some of whom had been trained by Freud himself, the institute also grew more conservative and authoritarian. It tightened its entrance requirements, denying membership to such well-known but unorthodox analysts as Erich Fromm, who was refused because of his lack of a medical degree. Those who were admitted fought for control of the institute and argued over theoretical differences. The institute split into several warring factions.

Political philosopher Hannah Arendt immigrated to the United States from Germany in 1940. Like many expatriate intellectuals, she taught at New York's New School for Social Research.

Because the institute desperately needed her to help teach its burgeoning student body—with whom she was so popular—Horney's position as a training analyst remained relatively secure. But once again her theories came under fierce attack, eroding her influence as a senior member of the analytic community. She still received encouragement from the Washington-Baltimore Psychoanalytic Society and Institute, where she had continued teaching some classes, and from some of its former members who had moved north and joined the New York organization. Horney, Harry Stack Sullivan, Clara Thompson, and William Silverberg made up the institute's progressive faction, which called itself the Zodiac.

The group met often to discuss psychoanalysis and lend each other support.

Determined to advance the work she believed in, Horney continued to publish criticisms of Freud. A 1936 paper entitled "The Problem of the Negative Therapeutic Reaction" refuted Freud's theory that adult neuroses have their roots directly in the experiences of early childhood. Horney wrote that Freudian analyses of adult patients "which connect the present difficulties immediately with influences in childhood are scientifically only half truths and practically useless." Without denying the importance of childhood events, she asserted the significance of adult experiences. In the paper, she con-

Horney made frequent summertime trips to Maine's pristine coast. The tranquillity of her vacations provided relief from the intense professional activity of her daily life in New York.

cluded that "the attitudes we see in the adult patient are not direct repetitions or revivals of infantile attitudes, but have been changed in quality and quantity by the consequences which have developed out of the early experiences."

Horney's brand of revisionism continued to rankle conservative analysts, but despite widespread disapproval she pressed on with her work. In the spring of 1937 publisher Walter Norton released Horney's first book, *The Neurotic Personality of Our Time*. This summary of her New School lecture course explored the nature of neurosis, offering both a critique of Freud's views and Horney's alternative to them. As in her 1936 paper, the heart of the text is Horney's argument against Freud's theory that adult neuroses are "compulsive repetitions" of infantile psychosexual experiences.

Horney rejected Freud's assertion that all children experience certain universal formative events, such as the Oedipus complex and *sibling rivalry* (competition between brothers and sisters). Instead, she theorized that because boys and girls from different cultures, historical periods, economic classes, and families grow up in vastly different circumstances, they pass through vastly different developmental processes. Where Freud assumed that the Oedipus complex plays a role in every child's life, for instance, Horney asserted that the complex develops only in certain families within certain cultures. Because cultural factors color childhood experience to a very high degree, she said, they contribute significantly to the genesis of adult neuroses.

Horney agreed with Freud that the events of early childhood set the stage for later emotional problems, but she proposed a new dynamic for this process. Neuroses, she wrote, arise in adults whose basic anxiety predisposes them to psychological difficulties. This basic anxiety, which Horney described as the sense that one is alone and helpless in a hostile world, originates in childhood. But, wrote Horney, rather than arising from the instinctual conflicts that Freud believed dominate early development, basic anxiety springs from a child's feelings of insecurity. Specifically, when a child's parents cannot or will not give him or her the love needed, the child feels rejected by them. According to Horney, this sets off a sequence of psychological events that produces basic anxiety and, thus, neurosis, in the adult. Neurotics do not, as Freud claimed, obsessively relive their early traumas: They merely reflect the influence of such events.

Horney noted that each child's experience of rejection, anxiety, and neurosis, refracted through the lenses of culture and class, takes on a unique character. Later, the continuing influence of external factors determines which of many possible forms adult neurosis takes. Neurosis must therefore be defined differently from culture to culture, because "there is no such thing as a normal psychology that holds for all" people, Horney wrote. She illustrated her point with an example from Native American culture: "One would run great risk in calling an Indian boy psychotic because he told us he had visions in which he believed. In the particular culture of these Indians the experience of visions and hallucinations is regarded as a special gift." Accordingly, psychoanalytic theory must take cultural diversity into account.

Reviewers from fields other than psychoanalysis greeted *The Neurotic Personality of Our Time* enthusiastically. One critic praised Horney's attention to "the cultural relativity of all neurotic disturbances . . . the changing social circumstances that have no small part in determining the battlefield where human impulses clash." Even Franz Alexander, Horney's old Chicago foe, applauded what he called her "independent, scrutinizing attitude, uninfluenced by accepted abstractions." But most reactions from the psychoanalytic mainstream were hostile. Horney had criticized Freudian theory on a deeper level than she had ever dared before. Few of her colleagues could accept such radical thinking.

Nonetheless, Horney's credentials prevented her critics from discrediting her entirely. A few, however, tried to find other ways to sully her reputation. Horney's daughter Renate had returned to Nazi Germany to marry, and Brigitte Horney had risen to stardom in the German film industry. Brigitte's position of prominence under Nazi rule (she made 27 films between 1930 and 1943) prompted rumors that she, and possibly her mother, had connections in the regime of Führer Adolf Hitler. Unlike many of her fellow expatriates, Karen Horney had never publicly condemned the Third Reich, and she had traveled to Germany in 1936 and 1937 to visit her daughters. Speculation about Horney's political allegiance rippled through the analytic world.

Horney dismissed the rumors as meaningless gossip, and her actions soon silenced most of her detractors. She placed distance between herself and her homeland, filing in 1937 for divorce from Oskar Horney, who harbored some Nazi sympathies. (The final papers came through in 1939.) She became a naturalized citizen of the United States in 1938, the year that Hitler marched into Austria and declared it part of Germany. As the führer expanded his empire, invading Poland in September 1939, Horney helped Renate and her husband escape Germany and settle in Mexico. That year, she also published her own views on fascism.

In a paper entitled "Can You Take a Stand?" Horney answered those who had faulted her for failing to take a public stance against the Nazis. She opened the paper with an analysis of the psychological attributes—fear and insecurity—that keep people, including herself, from standing up for the things they believe in. Suggesting that these characteristics "constitute a danger," Horney wrote that "it is people with these traits that succumb most easily to Fascist propaganda." Such individuals, she said, would rather follow than lead, and "Fascist ideology promises to fulfill all their needs" for structure and direction in their life. By contrast, "Democratic principles uphold the independence and strength of the individual. . . . Everyone convinced of the

value of Democracy should do his utmost to strengthen self-confidence and will power, and to develop individual capacity for forming judgements and making decisions."

Horney's paper may have quieted criticisms of her politics, but her second book, published shortly afterward,

Brigitte Horney appears in a scene from her 1934 film Liebe, Tod und Teufel *(Love, Death, and the Devil). The actress enjoyed wide popularity in Germany throughout the 1930s.*

once again angered the analytic community. *New Ways in Psychoanalysis,* a point-by-point assessment of Freudian theory and psychoanalytic technique, shocked many of Horney's colleagues even more than had *The Neurotic Personality of Our Time.* The book so upset orthodox analysts that they dropped their last pretenses of intellectual tolerance. Instead of merely dismissing Horney's theory as a misguided effort at revision, they now condemned it as a heretical attempt to overturn Freudian theory.

As a desperate German populace embraced nazism in the 1930s, fascist ideology inspired extreme nationalism. Many German youths joined patriotic organizations such as this drum corps.

Within two years of the publication of *New Ways in Psychoanalysis*, the New York Psychoanalytic Institute voted to strip Horney of all but a few duties. Horney and four supporters walked out of the April 1941 meeting where that vote took place and, two days later, submitted a letter of resignation. In the letter, the five analysts deplored the deterioration of the institute, where "reverence for dogma [established opinion] has replaced free inquiry; academic freedom has been abrogated [abolished]." Horney and her allies wrote that "we are interested only in the scientific advancement of psychoanalysis in keeping with the courageous spirit of its founder, Sigmund Freud." If she could not do this work at the New York Psychoanalytic Institute, Karen Horney would found an institute of her own.

After publishing two books, Horney found her position at the New York Psychoanalytic Society (pictured) increasingly intolerable. Ostracized by Freudian loyalists, she eventually resigned.

After breaking with the New York Psychoanalytic Society, Karen Horney eagerly embarked on the next stage of her career: founding her own psychoanalytic organization.

SEVEN

"Liberation and Growth"

In the weeks following their resignation from the New York Psychoanalytic Society and Institute, Karen Horney and her supporters wasted no time setting up their new organization, the Association for the Advancement of Psychoanalysis (AAP). The five defectors drafted a constitution outlining the association's philosophy and goals and elected their first president, William Silverberg. A Horney associate from the now-defunct Zodiac psychoanalytic group, Silverberg was happy to accept the nomination to head the rebel group; like them, he believed that "what Freud has founded has already become greater than Freud." Horney, who had no desire to govern the association herself, was pleased with the choice too. She felt that Silverberg's presidency would dispel any suspicion that the AAP was to serve as a platform for her views alone.

Even without an official title, Horney played a central role in the organization's activities right from the start. Her ties to the New School for Social Research helped her arrange for members of the association to teach courses there. But she found that she no longer wielded influence in the analytic mainstream. At the annual meeting of the American Psychoanalytic Association (APA), the national body that oversaw analytic activity in the United States, Horney tried but failed to convince the organization to recognize the new group. The APA stood firmly behind its New York chapter in ruling that "such moot [debatable] points of view" as Horney's had "no place in the preliminary basic training" of psychoanalytic candidates. The analytic establishment would not sanction the training of young analysts in non-Freudian techniques: The Association for the Advancement of Psychoanalysis was on its own.

But Horney and her colleagues did not wish to isolate themselves from the rest of the analytic community. In an effort to win support from individual psychoanalysts, the group sent a letter to each of the members of the APA explaining the reasons for their resignation. The letter asserted that the psychoanalytic community encompassed two schools of thought. The "classical" school, to which the APA belonged, accepted the "concepts and techniques . . . handed down by Freud" as the only true form of analysis. Horney's new organization, according to the letter, belonged to a "neo-classical" school. This school believed that analysis was "in an experimental stage of development, full of uncertainties, full of problems, to which anything approaching final and conclusive answers is still to be sought." The letter announced that the AAP proposed to seek those answers.

Although the letter appeared to make little impression on the country's analysts, the AAP soon began to grow. Fourteen recent graduates of the New York Psychoanalytic Institute resigned from the conservative organization to join the fledgling group. Six others from Washington, Detroit, and Chicago added their names to the roster of membership. Harry Stack Sullivan, a senior member of the New York Psy-

choanalytic, switched his allegiance to the AAP, and Erich Fromm became an honorary member. When, in the summer of 1941, the association established a training branch called the American Institute for Psychoanalysis, students—including Horney's daughter Marianne—quickly filled the new institute's classes.

By the time the AAP held its first annual meeting in May 1942, enrollment in the institute swelled to almost 30 candidates. The entire organization was off to a flying start, maintaining not only rapid growth but scientific vitality. To encourage a broad-based outlook among its members, the association regularly invited outside speakers such as Margaret Mead and Franz Alexander to deliver special lectures. Most of the group—from senior members to beginning candidates—also participated in frequent informal meetings where they freely discussed topics ranging from psychoanalysis to the visual arts. And in keeping with the group's commitment to diversity, all its senior members, including Horney, taught at the institute.

In addition to training candidates and overseeing the activities of the association, Horney served as the dean of the institute, taught at the New School and at New York Medical College, saw patients, and continued with her own writing. Throughout 1941 she concentrated on her third book, *Self-Analysis*, which was based on a course she had given at the New School. The book presents a refinement of Horney's theory of neurosis and proposes ways that psychoanalytic patients can supplement therapy on their own. Horney had engaged in self-analysis for most of her life, and in *Self-Analysis* she expressed her belief in its value. "Recognition of self," she wrote, "is as important as the recognition of other factors in the environment; to search for truth about self is as valuable as to search for truth in other areas of life."

Not surprisingly, *Self-Analysis* provoked the wrath of most psychoanalysts. They wrongly accused Horney of suggesting that people could analyze themselves without the assistance of trained professionals. One critic thundered that "Dr. Horney carries her rejection of Freud's theories about as far as it can go. . . . She propounds the belief that by adapting the techniques of regular analysis a neurotic person can effectually analyze himself." The interpretation was inaccurate and the response exaggerated, but most of the analytic community agreed that Horney had again gone too far. Nonetheless, Horney remained extremely popular among nonanalysts, and her services were in greater demand than ever.

The June 1942 publication of *Self-Analysis* coincided with another act of analytic rebellion. That month, a group of 14 analysts resigned from the New York Psychoanalytic Society to found the Columbia Psychoanalytic Clinic. Their letter of resignation echoed the one that Horney's group had submitted a year earlier. It described the society's "rigidity . . . generally stifling atmosphere . . . [b]ickering, slander and gos-

Horney invited anthropologist Margaret Mead, whose work on culture and psychology paralleled her own, to lecture at the American Institute for Psychoanalysis.

sip . . . [and] undercurrents of rivalry and disharmony." The AAP, it seemed, was not alone in its dissatisfaction with the psychoanalytic establishment.

Nor was the analytic world alone in its upheaval. World War II now raged across the globe: The Germans had swept through Europe and into the Soviet Union while the Japanese struggled to achieve dominance in the Pacific and the British fought with the Italians for control of North Africa. The United States had entered the fray after the December 7, 1941, bombing of Pearl Harbor, Hawaii, by Japanese forces. As the international conflict escalated and the Allies (the United States, France, Great Britain, and the Soviet Union) mobilized to defeat the Axis powers (Germany, Italy, and Japan), the AAP sought ways to make its own contribution. Horney and her colleagues formed a War Efforts Committee to publish bulletins on the psychology of war. Horney wrote two of these papers, one

Hitler's invasion of Poland ignited World War II in 1939. The war halted Horney's visits with her daughter Brigitte in Germany and disrupted their communication by telephone and letter.

analyzing the phenomenon of panic, the other describing the effects of war on children.

Of course, Horney took a personal as well as a professional interest in the war. Her daughter Brigitte, now married to a cameraman, still lived in Berlin, where conditions worsened each day. The Nazis, who had previously allowed the German film industry to operate fairly freely, had begun to clamp down on actors and directors who strayed from Nazi ideology. When film star Joachim Gottschalk, a close friend of Brigitte Horney, committed suicide with his family rather than obey Nazi orders to divorce his Jewish wife, Brigitte Horney was one of the few bold enough to attend his funeral. This defiant act brought her under Nazi suspicion, but she would not heed her mother's pleas to flee Germany for good. Not until a bout with tuberculosis forced her to a spa in Switzerland did Brigitte Horney leave the country.

Karen Horney had no such worries about her middle daughter. Marianne Horney had married in early 1942, adding not only a son-in-law but a best friend to her mother's life. Marianne's mother-in-law, Gertrude Lederer-Eckardt, had a physiotherapy practice in New York City. Horney and Eckardt met when, on Marianne's advice, the analyst consulted the physiotherapist about some back pain that troubled her. The two women liked each other immediately and soon became good friends. Within months Eckardt had signed on as Horney's secretary and all-around assistant. The close, produc-

In her later years, Horney's interests broadened to include oil painting and Eastern philosophy. She was particularly fascinated by Zen Buddhism.

tive personal and professional relationship would last until Horney's death.

Horney made a number of other friends during the early 1940s, including Richard Hulbeck, an artist who had fled Germany. Hulbeck encouraged Horney to pursue oil painting, a hobby she had recently acquired. Recalling the weekly lessons that he gave her, Hulbeck later remarked that Horney "definitely had talent and great intelligence." He also noted that in the early

Gertrude Lederer-Eckardt met Karen Horney in 1942. She went to work as Horney's secretary and became her confidante and constant companion.

1940s Horney "gave the impression of being at some personal turning point . . . between Fromm's ideologies and existentialism." It seemed to Hulbeck that Horney had arrived at "something like the idea that life wasn't really the outcome of your relationships with your parents but of your ability to handle it without neurotic symptoms."

At this turning point, Horney met Daisetz Suzuki, a world-renowned Zen Buddhist scholar. Suzuki introduced Horney to Zen, a spiritual discipline most widely practiced in Japan. Zen adherents seek *satori*—momentary enlightenment—through meditation.

Arrived at intuitively, satori is a highly personal, nonrational form of understanding that differs for each individual who experiences it. Neither religious ritual nor intellectual effort play a large part in the pursuit of satori. Instead, self-discipline and communion with nature prepare the Zen practitioner for the flash of insight. Zen appealed to Horney because it rejected rigid doctrine and systems of rules in favor of the search for self-evident truth. The analyst began to seek psychological insight in Zen philosophy.

Unfortunately, the freedom from doctrine that drew Horney to Zen no longer characterized the scientific organization she had helped found. Ideological disagreements now plagued the AAP and its institute, dividing the membership into two opposing groups. The AAP's first serious internal conflict centered around the question of whether lay analysts—those without medical credentials—should teach at the institute. Because she believed that the scientific community had greater respect for medically trained analysts, Horney opposed lay analysis. But her longtime friend and colleague Erich Fromm had practiced psychoanalysis for years without ever earning a medical degree—he had even analyzed Marianne Horney Eckardt. He felt that medical training should not be a prerequisite for an analytic career.

Horney and Fromm, who had previously supported each other in battles against the psychoanalytic establishment, now clashed in a battle for control of the AAP. In the end, Fromm and seven other members resigned, as did several of the institute's candidates. Soon afterward, another dispute arose at the AAP, leading to the resignation of six more members. By the middle of 1944, only 13 members remained, and 5 of those were serving in the military. That fall, even Marianne Horney Eckardt resigned.

The upheaval concerned Horney but did not discourage her. She described it as "growing pains" in a letter to a friend and expressed her determination to do what was best for the AAP. "This group is part of my life work," she said. She would not give it up so easily—nor would she abandon psychoanalysis, no matter how difficult a course lay ahead for her. In a paper, Horney confessed her love for her chosen profession, likening herself to a sailor with a favorite boat, who "loves it regardless of any deficiencies it may have." Rather than throw up her hands in the midst of difficulty, she transformed hard times into a lesson. She began to discuss the psychology of conflict in her lectures at the New School and soon started work on her fourth book, *Our Inner Conflicts*.

Our Inner Conflicts presents Horney's theory that all neurosis springs from the unsuccessful attempt to resolve certain inner conflicts. Horney had shown in her earlier books how emotional disharmony has its roots in the basic anxiety developed in childhood. The feelings of isolation, helplessness, and hostility that constitute this anxiety breed the neurotic trends of adulthood. In *Our Inner Conflicts*,

Horney explains how those trends compete with each other for dominance over the psyche. As they strive to find solutions to this internal discord, neurotic individuals assume one of three personality types.

Each of the three personalities seeks relief from its emotional pain. The *compliant* type moves toward others in a search for reassurance of love and acceptance. The *aggressive* type prefers to control others and enjoy the prestige that comes with dominance. The *detached* type maintains psychological

Although he had long maintained a warm friendship and fruitful professional relationship with Horney, Erich Fromm resigned from the AAP over theoretical differences.

distance from others, hoping to avoid the emotional honesty that intimacy requires. These neurotic individuals have four techniques for defending themselves against their psychical conflicts. Repression of some aspect of the personality can remove a source of conflict, while distancing the self from its emotions can remove the conflict from awareness. A third option is to construct an idealized image of the self and focus attention on that creation instead of on the *real self*. Finally, the neurotic may externalize sensations of disharmony, blaming outside factors for internal problems.

Inevitably, wrote Horney, these neurotic "solutions" of deep-seated problems do not work. The neurotic person may try to relieve stress through other means, such as ignoring or rationalizing internal contradictions, exerting rigid control over emotions, or adopting a cynical attitude. But unless a real solution is found, inner conflict will have unwanted consequences. The individual may be plagued by feelings of fear, depression, hopelessness, or despair or may become egocentric, overly sensitive, or cruel to others. According to Horney, the psychoanalyst's task is to reveal the neurotic inner conflicts to the patient and to help the patient discover the real self. With the discovery of the real self, said Horney, the patient will have "the capacity to learn from his experiences—that is, if he can examine his share in the difficulties that arise, understand it, and apply the insight to his life."

Like her mother, Marianne Horney Eckardt entered a career in psychoanalysis. A onetime member of the AAP, she ultimately chose to pursue her work outside Horney's circle of influence.

As she refined her own theories, Horney rejected Freud's tragic outlook on human psychology. Her work, wrote one critic, bears "an unmistakable hint of optimism."

Published in May 1945, *Our Inner Conflicts* received good reviews from most critics. One critic wrote that "there is an unmistakable hint of optimism in [Horney's] analysis, since she sees the personality as a going concern, capable of progressive adjustment." Horney's conviction that people can overcome their neuroses and that psychoanalysis can be a significant part of this process pervaded all the work she did in her final years.

Soon after *Our Inner Conflicts* appeared, Horney discussed her philosophy of optimism in an address to her colleagues. She reiterated her rejection of Freud's pessimistic view that "man is at bottom driven by elemental instincts of sex, greed, and cruelty," as she put it. "Man has potentialities for good and evil," she said, "and we see that he does develop into a good human being if he grows up under favorable conditions of warmth and respect for his individuality.... Psychoanalysis has become for us a means for liberation and growth as a human being." Horney's essential optimism regarding human psychology distinguished her from Freudian theorists perhaps more than any other single element of her thinking.

Passing through Hawaii on her way to Japan, Horney sports a lei. The analyst traveled to Japan shortly before her death, hoping to learn more about Zen Buddhism.

EIGHT

"The Best of Freudians"

In May 1945, the same month that Karen Horney published *Our Inner Conflicts*, the Russian army captured Berlin. A few days later Germany surrendered to the Allied forces, ending the war in Europe. Along with the rest of the world, Horney breathed a sigh of relief—and she had especially good reasons for doing so. In the months leading up to the fall of the Nazis, communications in Europe had been in such disarray that Brigitte Horney had lost touch with her mother. Some American newspapers had mistakenly reported the actress's death, and Brigitte had not been able to assure her mother of her safety. But as soon as telephone service was restored Karen Horney rushed a call through to Switzerland and reached her daughter.

Horney turned 60 on September 15, 1945, a month after World War II ended with the Japanese surrender. As busy as

ever with teaching responsibilities and her private practice, Horney still found time to relax. She liked to spend summer weekends at her Long Island beach house with her cocker spaniel Butschy and Gertrude Lederer-Eckardt. Once a year she traveled to Mexico to visit her daughter Renate, and after the fighting in Europe stopped she regularly visited Brigitte in Switzerland. Horney's enjoyment of oil painting, as well as her interest in Zen Buddhism and other spiritual and philosophical matters, enriched the analyst's limited leisure time.

Following the conclusion of World War II, the AAP recovered from its "growing pains" and in May 1946 marked its fifth anniversary. By then, enrollment at the institute had risen to 40 students and the association sponsored a wide array of scientific activity. The institute's faculty kept busy not only with teaching and research but with writing and publishing. Six of the AAP's senior members, including Horney, collaborated on a book, *Are You Considering Psychoanalysis?* Published in late 1946, the volume consists of several essays intended to answer the questions commonly asked by people thinking of entering psychoanalysis. Horney edited the volume and contributed two pieces to it: "What Does the Analyst Do?" and "How Do You Progress After Analysis?"

But Horney preferred writing on her own. She had already begun assembling her last book, *Neurosis and Human Growth*, which contains a complete summary of her theory of the origins and structure of neurosis. Earlier, in *Our Inner Conflicts*, Horney had described four basic ways that neurotic individuals attempt to resolve their fundamental internal tensions. Now, she focused her attention on one of those coping strategies, for she had come to the conclusion that all neuroses share a single source. Her new theory held that the creation of and belief in an unrealistic self-image is the fundamental fact of neurosis.

Psychologists have long known that children often retreat into fantasy in response to painful experiences. Children's fantasies sometimes include imagining themselves as perfect beings, a process Horney referred to as *self-idealization*. As long as the child keeps these fantasies in perspective, they serve an important purpose in emotional growth. The healthy child follows a course of *self-realization*—

discovering and developing the real self—to well-adjusted adulthood, with self-idealization playing only a small role. However, when self-idealization replaces self-realization as the primary mode of functioning, and when the individual continues compulsively to dwell on the fantasy self, this activity becomes the source of adult neurosis.

Because self-idealization creates an unrealistic self-image, it distances individuals from their real self. The discrepancy between fantasy and reality produces internal tension because neurotics cannot reconcile the differences between their contrasting identities. As Horney put it, "in all neurotic developments, alienation from the self is the nuclear problem." This alienation gives rise to and perpetuates neurosis in a number of ways.

Neurotic people want others to perceive them as the perfect beings they believe they are. When others do not cooperate in their fantasy, they are indignant at what they perceive as the world's injustice. Feeling abused and angry toward the world, neurotics experience a wide range of social problems. But not only do they have difficulty living with others, they also have difficulty living with themselves. Since neurotics base their sense of self-worth on an unrealistic self-image, their vanity is easily wounded. The false pride harbored by neurotic individuals crumbles whenever the harsh light of reality proves that their pride has little basis in fact.

Neurotics thus hate their real self for falling short of their idealized image of self. Self-hate permeates their psyche, destroying any chance they might have of making peace with themselves. Thus they seek to relieve their internal stress through various complex means. In their efforts to do so, neurotics generally take on one of three basic personality types. Building from the three neurotic types she presented in *Our Inner Conflicts*, Horney now termed these personality types the neurotic

major solutions to psychic pain. The first major solution is to repress the real self and identify entirely with the ideal self; the second is to identify with the real self and focus on its inferiority to the ideal self; the third is to remove oneself entirely from all conflict.

In the first case, the individual adopts what Horney calls an *expansive* personality. Expansive neurotics are narcissistic, self-centered, perfectionist, arro-

Zen scholar Daisetz Suzuki (left) accompanied Horney on her trip to Japan. Suzuki spoke of Horney as "one of the most wonderful persons."

gant, vindictive, and controlling. This solution contrasts with the second neurotic personality type. *Self-effacing* neurotics feel abused by others but thrive on suffering, self-sacrifice, and dependence. They fear success and do not like to assert themselves in situations of conflict. The third category of neurotic is the *resigned* type, who in order to avoid pain remains detached from others and from the self. Resigned neurotics value calmness, privacy, and independence and resent external authority.

Horney believed that therapy could help people move beyond the major solutions. Psychoanalysts, she felt, can help patients by disillusioning them; that is, by showing them that their idealized self-images are only fantasies. Once patients understand this, they no longer need neurotic solutions, because their internal conflict dissipates. With the obstructions to real personal growth removed, they can work toward self-realization. In describing the results of a successful analysis, Horney defined her notion of the healthy human being. "Having begun to accept himself as he is, with his difficulties," she wrote, "he also accepts the work at himself as an integral part of the process of living."

Some Freudians criticized *Neurosis and Human Growth* for its rejection of Freud's notion that, in Horney's words, "man is doomed to dissatisfaction whichever way he turns." But most readers greeted the book as Horney's most important work. Sociologist Ashley Montagu noted that orthodox ana-

lysts might object to Horney's apparently "irreverent treatment of Freud," but he suggested that readers try to recognize the distinction between irreverence and intelligent criticism. "Horney admires and respects Freud and his achievement, but does not worship him," he wrote. In his opinion, *Neurosis and Human Growth* placed Horney "among the best of Freudians."

After the 1950 publication of *Neurosis and Human Growth*, Horney slowed her hectic pace. The institute had a student body of more than 60 and a teaching staff of 25, but Horney had begun to tire easily and to experience abdominal pain, sometimes quite severe. Brigitte Horney, recently divorced and worried about her mother's condition, moved from Switzerland to New York City to be near her. Horney finally consulted a doctor, but he could not make a diagnosis. Choosing to ignore the problem, the analyst continued with her work, turning more and more of her attention to Zen philosophy and its relevance to psychology.

Daisetz Suzuki, famed for his ability to interpret Zen for the Western mind, now lived in New York and taught at Columbia University. Horney began spending many hours with him, trying to learn as much as she could about Zen. She set up Zen discussion groups in her home and invited Suzuki to lecture at the institute. Soon, she started incorporating Zen ideas into her own work. At a symposium in April 1951, she delivered a speech in which she mentioned the similarity

Horney spent much of her time in Japan in and around the city of Kyoto, visiting Zen shrines, temples, and monasteries. She also took in a folk festival and a Kabuki theater performance.

between Zen Buddhist philosophy and the theory outlined in *Neurosis and Human Growth*. "Eastern philosophers . . . have always believed in the spiritual powers in man. . . . These powers develop as man stops violating his nature."

A few months later, Japanese psychiatrist Akahiso Kondo enrolled at the institute, where he met Horney. Kondo practiced Morita therapy, a Japanese form of psychotherapy rooted in Zen philosophy. Morita theory holds that egocentricity and alienation from nature are the primary causes of emotional imbalance. Patients can overcome their neuroses by engaging in certain activities related to Zen notions of proper human conduct. Morita therapy fascinated Horney, especially in its reliance on Zen principles. She decided to visit Japan and find out more about Japanese psychotherapy and Zen Buddhism.

In July 1952, Karen Horney set out for Japan with her daughter Brigitte Horney, Daisetz Suzuki, Suzuki's assistant, Akahiso Kondo, and two friends. The trip was intended, according to Horney, to give the travelers an opportunity "to study Japanese culture by getting into direct contact with people and places, by intensive discussion with a few well-selected persons, and by leisurely devoting time to the appreciation of nature." For one month the group visited Zen Buddhist monasteries and shrines, observing and speaking with Zen monks. Horney also met with Japanese psychiatrists and delivered a lecture on psychoanalysis at a Tokyo

By the end of her life, Horney's commitment to the field of psychoanalysis earned her a distinguished reputation, not only among her supporters but among her critics.

medical school. Her contact with the Japanese psychiatric community led her to the conclusion that Morita therapy, while valuable in many ways, was limited in its ability to resolve deep-rooted psychological problems.

By contrast, Horney's firsthand look at Zen Buddhism made her even more excited about it. Although she found few direct correlations between her theory and Zen philosophy, she believed that the two shared a similar spirit. She was thrilled to discover such parallels to her views as the Buddhist notion that "truth, in the sense of reality, cannot be cut up into pieces and arranged into a system." When she returned to the United States at the end of the summer, Horney drew heavily on Eastern thought in her ongoing work. For example, in her last paper, published just after her return from Japan, she expressed a Zen idea in her own terms: "Life is not a problem to be solved but an experience to be realized." The principle fit perfectly with her view of psychology.

Horney would not live to develop a Zen-informed version of psychoanalysis. In October she fell ill and entered a hospital, where doctors finally diagnosed her condition: cancer of the gall bladder. She recovered briefly, but late November found her in the hospital once again. Although "she knew she was dying," according to a young medical student assigned to her ward, Horney retained her optimism. The student later recalled that when he and Horney spoke about the difficulties that face women in medicine, she expressed the hope that "maybe when you reach my age the world will be quite different." Those were her last recorded words. On December 4, 1952, at the age of 67, Karen Horney died.

News of Horney's death shook the psychoanalytic community. Even her opponents praised her as a "distinguished, vigorous and independent figure" dedicated to the "thoroughgoing investigation of psychic conflict." But to her daughters and friends, to her associates at the AAP, and to the nearly 100 students at the institute, Horney had been more than just a brilliant scientist. Speaking at her funeral, theologian Paul Tillich said:

> She knew the darkness of the human soul, and the darkness of the world, but believed that what giveth light to any one suffering human being will finally give light to the world. The light she gave was not a cold light of passionless intellect, it was the light of passion and love. She wrote books but loved human beings. She helped them by insights into themselves which had healing power.

Theologian Paul Tillich, a longtime friend of Horney, eulogized the analyst at her funeral. He said that she was filled with "the light of passion and love."

Karen Horney's work has continued to impart healing power in the years since her death. The American Institute for Psychoanalysis, which her colleagues renamed The Karen Horney Psychoanalytic Institute and Center, still flourishes in New York City. All her books, which have been translated into 13 languages, remain in print. Together, they have sold more than a half-million copies worldwide. A collection of her early papers on feminine

After her death, Horney's colleagues renamed the American Institute for Psychoanalysis in her honor. The Karen Horney Psychoanalytic Institute still operates in New York City.

psychology was translated from German and published in 1967, making those works widely available to speakers of English. Many of her theories, ignored or rejected during her lifetime, have since been accepted and integrated into mainstream psychoanalysis as well as other branches of psychiatry. But more important, through the work of Karen Horney countless people around the world have found the strength to heal their life.

FURTHER READING

Appignanesi, Richard and Oscar Zarate. *Freud for Beginners.* New York: Pantheon Books, 1979.

Brenner, Charles. *An Elementary Textbook of Psychoanalysis.* New York: Anchor Press, 1974.

Freud, Sigmund. *Introductory Lectures on Psychoanalysis.* New York: Norton, 1966.

Horney, Karen. *The Adolescent Diaries of Karen Horney.* New York: Basic Books, 1980.

———, ed. *Are You Considering Psychoanalysis?* New York: Norton, 1946.

———. *Feminine Psychology.* New York: Norton, 1967.

———. *Neurosis and Human Growth.* New York: Norton, 1950.

———. *The Neurotic Personality of Our Time.* New York: Norton, 1937.

———. *New Ways in Psychoanalysis.* New York: Norton, 1939.

———. *Our Inner Conflicts.* New York: Norton, 1945.

———. *Self-Analysis.* New York: Norton, 1942.

Kelman, Harold. *Helping People: Karen Horney's Psychoanalytic Approach.* New York: Science House, 1971.

Quinn, Susan. *A Mind of Her Own: The Life of Karen Horney.* New York: Summit Books, 1987.

Rubins, Jack. *Karen Horney: Gentle Rebel of Psychoanalysis.* New York: Dial Press, 1978.

Westkott, Marcia. *The Feminist Legacy of Karen Horney.* New Haven: Yale University Press, 1986.

CHRONOLOGY

Sept. 15, 1885	Karen Clementina Theodora Danielsen born in Eilbek, Germany
1901	Registers for Gymnasium classes in Hamburg
1906	Enrolls at Ludovico Albertina University in Freiburg; meets Oskar Horney
1908	Studies at University of Göttingen
1909	Moves to Berlin; marries Oskar Horney; enrolls at the University of Berlin
1910	Undergoes psychoanalysis with Karl Abraham
1911	Gives birth to a daughter, Brigitte; joins the Berlin Psychoanalytic Society; begins psychiatric internship
1913	Gives birth to a daughter, Marianne
1915	Receives medical degree; starts work at Lankwitz Kuranstalt hospital; becomes an officer of the Berlin Psychoanalytic
1916	Gives birth to a daughter, Renate
1919	Opens private practice
1920	The Berlin Psychoanalytic launches its Poliklinik; Horney begins analyzing patients and training students there
1926	Karen and Oskar Horney separate
1926–32	Horney develops and refines her theory of feminine psychology; publishes 13 papers on the topic
1932	Arrives in the United States; cofounds the Chicago Institute for Psychoanalysis
1934	Moves to New York City; joins the New York Psychoanalytic Society and Institute
1937	Publishes *The Neurotic Personality of Our Time*
1938	Gains American citizenship
1939	Publishes *New Ways in Psychoanalysis*; finalizes divorce from Oskar Horney
1941	Resigns from the New York Psychoanalytic; founds the Association for the Advancement of Psychoanalysis (AAP) and its training arm, the American Institute for Psychoanalysis
1942	Publishes *Self-Analysis*
1945	Publishes *Our Inner Conflicts*
1946	Horney and five colleagues publish *Are You Considering Psychoanalysis?*
1950	Horney publishes *Neurosis and Human Growth*
1952	Travels to Japan
Dec. 4, 1952	Karen Horney dies at the age of 67
1967	Publication of *Feminine Psychology*

INDEX

Constance Jones, senior editor of the AMERICAN WOMEN OF ACHIEVEMENT series, is the author of three previous books on various topics. She holds a bachelor's degree in economics and political science from Yale University.

Matina S. Horner is president of Radcliffe College and associate professor of psychology and social relations at Harvard University. She is best known for her studies of women's motivation, achievement, and personality development. Dr. Horner serves on several national boards and advisory councils, including those of the National Science Foundation, Time Inc., and the Women's Research and Education Institute. She earned her B.A. from Bryn Mawr College and Ph.D. from the University of Michigan, and holds honorary degrees from many colleges and universities, including Mount Holyoke, Smith, Tufts, and the University of Pennsylvania.